The Supernova
Multiplier

The Supernova Multiplier

7 STRATEGIES FOR FINANCIAL ADVISORS TO GROW THEIR PRACTICES

Rob Knapp

WILEY

Published by John Wiley & Sons, Inc., Hoboken, New Jersey.

Published simultaneously in Canada.

For general information on our other products and services or for technical support, please contact our Customer Care Department within the United States at (800) 762–2974, outside the United States at (317) 572–3993, or fax (317) 572–4002.

Wiley publishes in a variety of print and electronic formats and by print-on-demand. Some material included with standard print versions of this book may not be included in e-books or in print-on-demand. If this book refers to media such as a CD or DVD that is not included in the version you purchased, you may download this material at http://booksupport.wiley.com. For more information about Wiley products, visit www.wiley.com.

Library of Congress Cataloging-in-Publication Data

Names: Knapp, Rob
Title: The supernova multiplier : 7 strategies for financial advisors to grow their practices / Robert D. Knapp.
Description: Hoboken, New Jersey : John Wiley & Sons, Inc., [2019] | Includes index. |
Identifiers: LCCN 2018045782 (print) | LCCN 2018047876 (ebook) | ISBN 9781119539773 (ePub) | ISBN 9781119539810 (Adobe PDF) | ISBN 9781119539803 (hardcover)
Subjects: LCSH: Investment advisors. | Investment advisor-client relationships. | Financial planners. | Financial services industry—Customer services.
Classification: LCC HG4621 (ebook) | LCC HG4621 .K643 2019 (print) | DDC 332.6068/4—dc23
LC record available at https://lccn.loc.gov/2018045782

Cover image: Wiley
Cover design: © titoOnz/iStock.com

Printed in the United States of America

V10006880_121818

Contents

Foreword

When Larry Wilson wrote Rob Knapp's Foreword for *The Supernova Advisor*, Larry stated, "Rob and his team have a PhD in the hard knocks school of leaders leading change. Better yet, they transformed what they learned into a powerful change system called Supernova."

A lot has happened to Rob and his Supernova Consulting Group since those heady days of transforming chaos to process using the Supernova model. The model has evolved and become the service model of thousands of Financial Advisory teams throughout the world. Having that eagle-eye view across the industry has given Rob a unique perspective. Rob Shaffer, Supernova coach and friend of the author for over 30 years, said it best, "If I only knew then [when he was managing offices] what I know now, what a difference I could have made." Rob Knapp successfully shares that experience in *The Supernova Multiplier*".

This book picks up where *The Supernova Advisor* left off. If you haven't read the first book, don't worry, Knapp gives you a quick summary in the introduction. Rob reviews the Supernova process of segmentation and organization, gives you numerous updated and improved ideas, and then dives into acquisition.

Growing practices has been the biggest challenge of the modern financial services industry. Knapp takes on that challenge by offering the 7 strategies for Growth, with real-life examples, testimonials, and key takeaways for each strategy. Nowhere has anyone gone into so much detail on exactly how to step-by-step transform your chaotic acquisition strategy to one that is based on a Supernova process. As a former Naval Aviator, Knapp believes in plan, process, and rituals. He literally gives you checklists to follow as you go from one strategy to the next.

Knapp will show you why some financial advisor's (FA's) with similar talent, experience, and drive are successful using these models while others never get the results. How many times have we heard, "I've tried using [COIs, Boards, Networking groups], but I never get any referrals." Rob interviews numerous FAs who in their own words tell you their secrets to breaking through those barriers.

Rob will not only get you on the right path, but show you how to build in the rituals and accountability tools to keep you on track. How many times have you heard, "I used to do that and it really worked, but I don't do it now." This FA has no real rituals built into the system and no accountability. Plato said, "learning is remembering." Just because something sounds familiar doesn't mean you really understand how it will benefit you in modern-day marketing. Open your mind and let these ideas in. Knapp stated, "I haven't held anything back here. I have put every good idea from the last ten years of coaching and my 45 years in the world of sales and marketing into this book." For Rob this book was a labor of love. Taking over three years to create, with hundreds of interviews and thousands of coaching hours, Rob has learned as much from his students as he has taught. Rob intends to donate all proceeds to his foundation, which is dedicated to educating those less fortunate, as he has done with his previous books.

Now dive into *The Supernova Multiplier* with the mindset of an eager learner and this will be as transformational as any journey you have ever taken.

Steve Siebold, author,
Secrets Self-Made Millionaires Teach Their Kids

Acknowledgments

The *Supernova Multiplier* was created out of a desire to share everything we have learned since we began the Supernova Consulting Group in 2006. That is a tall order. We interviewed over 100 Financial Advisors (FAs) who went through our year-long coaching program and showed tremendous growth. We could not include them all in this book but rather used several examples for each of the 7 Strategies for Growth. Their contribution to this book gave it credibility. Their creativity in adapting these ideas to their practice gave us some exceptional breakthroughs. Let me first thank Bob Mulholland who gave us permission to speak to both his staff and Financial Advisors. His leadership, first at Merrill Lynch and then at another major financial services firm, gave our program tremendous credibility. He encouraged us to roll out Supernova to all regions of his firm. Not once but again two years later. We trained over 3,000 Financial Advisors and their teams. We trained their top managers and saw the program get tremendous traction and success. Bob has since retired, but his legacy lives on. The FA satisfaction rate went from the low 30s to the 80s during his tenure. An outstanding accomplishment. Critical players on his team who became completely immersed in the program were Heather Gifford, Gerry Schreck, Chuck Patton, Greg Staab, Clay Bedford, and Dick Lown. Many of these professionals were out in the field with our team coordinating, presenting, and supporting, and coaching the program. Some of their words appear in the text of this book.

Financial Advisors who adopted the Supernova model, gave testimonials in front of their peers, and were interviewed for this book include Ken Shapiro, Tom Laviccaro, Luke Wiley, Alissa Quinn, Rob Benoit, Rick Rogers, Laurie Barry, Greg Kadet, Hugh Stephenson, Kim Jenson, Brad Desormeau,

Ben Tarantino, Kevin McGrath, Patrick Renn, Cromwell Baum, Hugh Stephenson, John Hurlow, and Michael Beers.

Tom Anderson went so far as to contribute a whole chapter to the book. Bill Cates offered his expertise on "Getting More Referrals Now," mastermind groups and networking. I will be eternally grateful to my team at Supernova who helped create content, coached thousands of teams, and gave overall support to this book. They are Rob Shaffer, Curtis Brown, Stan Craig, Lori Showley, and Rob Kennedy. I relied on others for their counsel and expertise especially Jim McEnerney, Jim Guthrie, and Rick Knapp.

Editing was done by Cindy Beuoy, Jennifer Werner, Greg Perry, Courtney Knapp, and Marcia Knapp. Thanks to the team from Wiley who did the final editing and pulled all the pieces together.

A special thanks goes to my friend and business associate, Cindy Beuoy, who was the driving force behind this work. When I would fall behind my timeline, she would always be there to get me back on track. In the final 36 hours she edited for 18 hours. Her passion for the work, the mission, and this book is something very special. We have done two books in the last 12 months and that is no easy feat.

Finally, a big thank you to my wife Marcia who puts up with my long hours and days of travel and shares our mission of "Improving the client experience worldwide by improving the FA experience."

As with *The Supernova Advisor*, all proceeds of this book will go to The Knapp Family Foundation, whose mission is to make available education to those who might not be able to afford it.

Introduction

One of the most significant joys of my life continues to be helping high performers push through to even greater achievements, and yes, "push through" is the right way to describe the effort. Professionals who are already operating at the higher levels of production have long ago mastered the fundamentals and put in place practices, habits, and rituals that consistently propel them to the top. They attract the best clients. They build the most productive networks.

High performers are the 20% who deliver 80% of everything that's good: new money, better clients, sharper staff. It's no easy thing to guide them to an even higher realm. This push through encompasses three elements: coaching that's close and invested, a commitment strong enough to endure plateaus and even setbacks, and, most of all, it requires a model . . . a framework that builds success and tools that are precisely calibrated to the specific demands of exceptional performance.

In the world of advising high-net-worth clients, that model is Supernova.

Supernova emerged from the dual crisis of the bear market of the early 2000s and the growing dissatisfaction of the clients we served—or, more precisely, didn't serve very well. A group of phenomenal individuals and I built Supernova to answer a simple but surprisingly complex question: What does it take to deliver the ultimate client experience?

Evolution of Supernova

A bit of background to give those new to Supernova a quick overview of the model. I wrote *The Supernova Advisor* in 2007 and Wiley published it in 2008. While this book is written as a stand-alone resource, reading *The Supernova Advisor* may offer you broader and deeper understanding of the model. Heck, even if you did read it, take another look. Landing at just over 100 pages, it's not going to take long to reconnect with the core ideas we previously presented:

- It all begins with a financial plan. Implementing that plan is the key. It is indeed an ongoing process that never ends.
- The 80/20 Rule defines your book of business more effectively than any other principle. That is, 20% of your clients give you 80% of your income. Having more clients doesn't change that; it just means you're working more and delivering less.
- The ultimate client experience is not the result of great products or your brilliant investment strategy. Ultimate experiences are assembled, call by call, meeting by meeting, in the form of regular and scheduled contact. We call it 12-4-2. Twelve scheduled contacts, one per month, four of which include a quarterly review of the full portfolio, and two 60-minute, face-to-face meetings with a broad but specific agenda. This is not a suggestion. This is the bedrock from which Supernova originates.
- The only way to maintain a 12-4-2 contact discipline is to reduce your book from 300 or 400 clients to about 100. That's the maximum number of clients you can serve. (You can add more if you want to work nights and weekends.) Every one of those clients has assets that equal or surpass a minimum you set. It is called segmentation with a min/max. And despite how it looks, it's also how you grow.
- Supernova inverts the org chart. Top-down, command/control is out. Administrators who set the calendar are now driving the day-to-day. Client files stay on paper and in folders. Everything is documented, which compliance just loves and so will you!
- A referable service model is not a certification you earn; it's a commitment you make. It's becoming the CFO for your clients, and it moves forward on expressing personal values, not just increasing asset value.

- New client acquisition happens organically, deliberately, and continually. A higher minimum is the first step, and exceptional service makes it possible. Pushing everything forward is a precise plan of networking specialization. And by "precise" we mean scheduled, and accountable.
- Leadership in a Supernova practice is about serving not directing. It's transparent. It's scheduled and measured every single day. Stewardship is a fine idea for a forest. In a Supernova practice, however, change and improvement are the oxygen everyone breathes. Without it, the practice will stagnate.

That's a Supernova lightning round. Know where your income comes from and structure your practice around it. **Contact** your clients on a predictable schedule with meaningful content. **Segment** your book into a manageable number. **Organize** the practice around the rhythm of regular client contact. **Plan** with your clients versus reacting to them or the financial markets. **Grow** the practice with a series of acquisition techniques that are both expansive in nature and regular in frequency. **Lead** by serving and by propelling change. Supernova is a transformative model for most Financial Advisors (FAs), and it can literally change your life. Supernova delivers a more productive and deeper relationship between advisors and their most profitable clients and has the added benefit of also making them richer. This model results in, at the minimum, slow and steady growth without fear of plateauing and at the maximum, a doubling or even tripling of your practice.

When I retired I felt Supernova was an enormously satisfying legacy to leave behind to others. I thought my job was done and I would be spending the rest of my days enjoying my family, hiking, golfing, fishing, and playing tennis. That was until my daughter Courtney reminded me of my mission statement "to go where no man has gone before and joyfully share the map." I was also hearing from friends, still in the field, some version of: "Supernova is too good—too important—to fade away in your absence." With my daughter's encouragement and my desire to give back to the industry I had devoted my life to, I decided I should write a book.

The Supernova Advisor was a how-to guide on implementing the Supernova Process, but what gave the book its heartbeat was not the practical guidance; it was the personal stories, including mine. Supernova was my awakening as a better advisor and leader. All along, I could see where I wanted my career to go but I didn't know there was a bridge right in front of me until my team and I took the first steps.

The first book is an inspiring collection of stories of advisors' lives changed for the better and their clients' true potential reached. I know they were inspiring because again and again, readers told me so. I was grateful and humbled to receive countless calls and notes brimming with appreciation. The reviews were fabulous. The book made a few "Best Of" lists. The first print run sold out, so did the second, and the third! And even if you don't read, or re-read, *The Supernova Advisor*, its final sentence tells you something important. After expressing my thanks for the extraordinary people who helped me shape the Supernova model, I ended it with:

And now, it's yours.

With that official handing over of the reins, I envisioned my post-publishing career as the benevolent architect of Supernova. My thinking was that while I would be speaking to big groups in big rooms about the process, the advisors who first implemented it would be sending a steady stream of validating anecdotes and comforting statistics my way. It was going to be many things . . . comfortable, satisfying, and mostly, hands-off.

And then, after I spoke at a national firm's annual meeting about Supernova, the firm approached me about coaching their advisors. Running a quirky little solo business after a long corporate career was not part of my plan. Then another firm requested a group of Supernova consultants to train their FAs and ended up integrating the Supernova Process into their practice management program nationwide.

I guess I could have said no. And maybe I would have if what I was seeing in the industry was more reassuring. Instead it was distressing, and that included the advisors who had initially embraced Supernova.

Readers of the first book will remember that we developed the model from iteration and experimentation, and then spread the word in big town hall-style meetings. We weren't there to coach Supernova; we had our own day jobs. For the most part, Supernova was a Do-It-Yourself undertaking, and as the saying goes: "your mileage may vary."

And vary it did. Once the book was out, some teams—not just Merrill, but across the industry—read it and somehow encoded Supernova beautifully into their organizational DNA. But they were by far the exception. Some tried to slice different genes onto the model and the results were predictably mutated. Others did their best with what they had and what they knew, but it wasn't enough. They needed a coach. And I wasn't going to watch as Supernova failed. I owed it to my original team and I owed it to myself. But mostly, I owed it to the advisors who, in growing desperation, had reached out to me and said, "We know this will work but we don't know how."

So, I built the Supernova Consulting Group by putting together a team of talented consultants who I trained to coach the program. We developed and refined a suite of coaching tools. I went from hands-off to over-my-head, and along the way I got inside the Supernova model more deeply than I ever had before. It offered me an important vantage point from which to view an emerging trend that was spreading quickly across practices in large firms and even small independents.

A tiered model of client service was quickly taking root. The categorization of clients, "A" clients, "B" clients, "C" clients, and so on. became prevalent. Different firms had different ways to define them, but the tiers were becoming the norm. It was a perverted kind of Supernova segmentation—no minimum, no maximum, all the disorder and difficulties of too many clients paying advisors too much for too little real advising. It's also critical to say this: Supernova could get better. By coaching teams up close, we saw that Supernova's Five Stars could be better aligned to unleash optimal results.

By watching practices grow, and fail to grow, we learned a whole new vocabulary of acquisition that puts giving at the center...not giving in order to receive, merely giving. Win/win is transactional thinking. Creating wins for everyone is the optimal mindset.

By serving leaders, we learned that we have much to learn about leadership, and learn we did.

Prepare to Meet the Multipliers

The Supernova Multiplier brings me back to my sweet spot: pushing high performers even higher, and from here on I will assume you are one of them. You are the difference makers, and you can also be challenging to coach. High performers may resist change if it contradicts their own instincts or even temporarily slows their ascent. I get it, and these pages will help you understand the "why" behind the "what." Everything I'll ask you to do has been proven successful, often spectacularly so.

High performers also create a kind of coaching jujitsu. I think I'm pushing them forward and they end up driving me forward. You'll meet many of those FAs and their teams in the pages ahead. It's with their help—and though their example—that I've crystallized the idea of multipliers.

A Supernova multiplier does exactly that: It (or they) multiplies an inherent strength within the Supernova model. Supernova multipliers can be practices and rituals. And Supernova multipliers can be people. Either way, it's not about incremental improvement—that would be a Supernova plus. I'm in the business of multiplying, and as a top performer, you are too.

In this book you will learn how to:

- Create multipliers to grow your practice (acquisition techniques)
- Measure performance and use of those multipliers (accountability)
- Apply the rule of reciprocity by giving to give not to get; and finally

- Develop an environment of trust within your practice and with your clients that differentiates you from the crowd and elevates you in an industry that is full of mistrust.

Let's Get to Work—If You're Not on the Path, You're Asleep

This book is working in two realms which might appear entirely different but are profoundly interrelated. So deeply in fact, that I don't separate them. One of the ambitions of this book is to deliver the same realization to you.

The first realm is that of actions: practices, rituals, conversations. This is the "doing" of what I've so often heard FA teams say to me "Yes, we do Supernova," and they might be right. They also might be fooling themselves—and more importantly their clients—into believing that once they crossed that bridge to a smaller book of business and did their best to keep client contact scheduled and regular, then the heavy lifting of Supernova was over. And if Supernova was about maintaining the status quo, they might be right. But Supernova is about growth, which brings us to the second realm, your mindset.

An optimal mindset is the beating heart of a growing Supernova practice. It's what my friend and mentor Larry Wilson called "playing to win, not just playing not to lose." The optimal mindset hums with an earned confidence in the value of what you offer and even who you are. It's a willing embrace of challenges large and small. It's the generosity to listen more than talk. It's a true understanding that leadership is service. It's love and trust conquering fear. The Supernova mindset is all this and more. Every action, practice, ritual, and conversation in the first realm is a physical extension of an optimal mindset.

The human dimension and growth potential within the Supernova mindset are incredible to behold, and life-changing to experience. And when I say "incredible" you should understand that I'm not leaning on the devalued definition that so many seem to have adopted, as in "this yogurt is awesome." No, I mean to inspire actual awe, which can be acutely lacking in teams and individuals that have reached a plateau and are comfortable staying there. To stop growing is to step off the path and fall asleep. Now we're back to the language of the hero's journey.

The hero's journey is different for every person. Each looks different from the outside and feels different from the inside. For some, maybe most, the hero doesn't even know they are on a journey. They are simply reacting to a series of challenging circumstances and trying their best to anticipate the next ones. It may not feel like a journey at all, and probably isn't even experienced as heroic. That doesn't diminish the transformative power of the experience. And, I don't want you to get too hung up on the word "hero."

Heroes rescue babies from burning buildings...heroes jump on the grenade so the rest of the unit can fight on...heroes are brave in the face of great danger. Well, yes, and there's more. It's so commonly heard that it's not much of an insight. When the news camera points at the people we've tagged as heroes they always protest "I was just reacting" or "I didn't do anything that any other person wouldn't do in that situation." Have you ever heard someone say, "Why thank you, yes, I am a hero"? We'd fall off our sofas if we saw that! And what if someone in the glare of the coverage said, "Well, this is all part of my journey...my hero's journey." It's not going to happen with true acts of selfless bravery, so why should I expect you to claim anything similar?

An average advisor may see themselves as many things—an ambitious striver, a frustrated cat herder, a fire fighter running between emergencies. A Supernova advisor probably envisions their life in more generous terms, such as trusted, invested, and empathic, but hardly intrepid, or heroic. And besides, a hero becomes a hero by besting an enemy or at least averting a deleterious force, right? There's a malicious force all right, and you face it every time you try to improve yourself, evolve your practice, and advance your team. It's called fear.

Fear fits itself between you and any forward action, and manifests itself in a thousand forms, many of which can sound quite reasonable. Any of these sound familiar?

My CSA is good, but I'm not sure it's right to put him/her in charge of setting every appointment.

I am going to keep my small accounts that pay me a fee. Why not? They never bother me.

Many of my clients don't want 12-4-2. They are too busy and I don't want to bother them.

I don't want to be pinned down to appointments for all my clients. I will just call them every month on my schedule.

I get the folders for our clients, but it's overkill to create one for every team member, every prospective client and every Center of Influence.

Centers of Influence don't work for us.

I'm uncomfortable asking for introductions.

Do those seem like inconsequential fears? Sure, maybe, but they are also diminishing the Supernova mindset and limiting your growth. Let's listen in on a truly toxic set of fears trying their best to sound reasonable:

"I don't have a process for asking my clients for introductions, I don't want to appear needy."

"If I ask for referrals my clients will think my business is struggling, and they'll hesitate to increase assets with us, or leave altogether."

"Social media is a waste of time."

All of this is Fear Talk. Fear of losing control. Fear of looking "too organized" and less of a "big thinker." Fear of being vulnerable. And the big one: Fear of feeling rejected. The fear of rejection—acknowledged or denied or lurking completely undetected—is the **single most common reason Supernova FAs and their practices fail to grow.** This is surprising for a population of professionals who have endured and emerged successfully from their early career days spent cold calling.

What gives?

Simply put, they've stepped off the path. They are asleep to the personal growth and professional adventure that follows when fears are acknowledged, faced, and conquered.

Resistance to the activities that power growth often disguises itself as busyness, or laziness, or even a smug complacency that values ego over risk. These aren't bad advisors and certainly not bad people. They've been lulled to sleep by the hum of a stable practice and fallen off the path. How about you? Are you on or off the path?

Don't answer that—yet.

How This Book Is Organized

The chapters in this book stand as singular invitations for you to consider. You can move through the book in chapter sequence, or you can zero in on chapters that call to you. Either way, I challenge you to maintain an open mind throughout. I speak directly and with candor about FAs who are failing to grow, but I'm not judging them, or you. My hope is that their stories will inspire you and motivate you to develop your own Supernova mindset.

We subtitled the book: *7 Strategies for a Financial Advisor to Grow Their Practice.* Each strategy will be addressed in an individual chapter, which will give the reader multipliers to accelerate their growth. Acquisition is an important facet of the Supernova Process and the fourth step in growing your practice.

In the Supernova Process, acquisition of new clients is based on "value given, value recognized," which simply means when you give a client or prospect a proactive service experience you will be giving them value they will recognize and reward you for with introductions to their friends and family.

Building your pipeline is a lot like preparing a gourmet meal. You first decide what you want to cook, assemble all the ingredients, carefully mix the ingredients together using spices or herbs for flavor, cook the dish in an oven or cooktop or grill, time the cooking so everything gets done at the same time, and watch so that your dinner is not overcooked.

In building your pipeline you decide on who your ideal clients are, meet them through a referral or common interest, show them how you can be of value to them, and if you are the "right mix," bring them "under the tent" by meeting with them regularly and possibly creating a cash flow analysis or plan for their future.

The Supernova Acquisition Strategies are based on relationships. If you are a rookie you know how important those first few relationships are. Even if they are small accounts you treat them like they are gold. You might call them more often, work on their risk tolerance and market strategy, take them out to dinner or host a client outing. As you acquire more clients you won't be able to spend as much time with each one. Supernova advisors schedule client meetings monthly.

It is important that you know how to describe your ideal client. Why? There are two reasons:

1. Doesn't it make sense that you know what you are looking for? If you know what you want you have a better chance of finding it? You could waste a lot of time looking for oranges in an apple orchard.
2. More important, you have to be able to tell referral sources what type of client you want. Have you ever gotten a referral that you didn't want? You keep that from happening by making sure that referral sources know what you want. If your minimum is $1 million, they aren't going to send you a $35,000 referral that in the past you have probably accepted because you didn't want to appear unappreciative.

There are two parts to your ideal client. The first is your minimum. You do not have time to provide a superior, Supernova level of service to everyone. Your minimum allows you to control the size of your practice.

The second part of the ideal client model is the very important "soft" issues. What are soft issues? They are things such as trust, likeability, following your advice, and treating your support staff well. The easiest way to find the soft issues most important to you is to look at the characteristics of your favorite clients; the ones you most enjoy.

The Supernova model is easy to remember: 90-6-4-2-2-1-1. The "90" stands for 90 days to convert a prospect to a client.

The "6" is for six Centers of Influence. The "4" stands for a four-person Mastermind Group. The "2" is for two Niches, the next "2" is community involvement and the first "1" is social networking and the second "1" is for "Value. Important. Permission. Suggestions. Advice" (VIPSA) or referrals. By design any of these strategies will result in new ideal clients. Don't feel overwhelmed thinking you need to do all of the strategies all of the time. Start with one or two and build them into your business model. Over time you can gradually add another one.

My passion is coaching high performers. I interview all prospective coaching clients to determine if they are a good fit for the program. Ideally, they show up ready to change and they demonstrate the most significant growth. I want to elevate every reader to a place where they can see the gaps in their performance (which is always a reflection of a sub-optimal mindset) and move to fill them. That's where the fun starts...that's where Supernova ignites exponential growth...that's where you rejoin the path and continue your journey.

The Supernova Multiplier

CHAPTER

1

Hitting the Wall

The Why Behind *The Supernova Multiplier*

Supernova coaching was initially delivered in a 12-week, or 90-day course. Essentially, the program consisted of three months of weekly calls, with plenty of content to consume and learn in the days between each call. It broke down like this: four weeks of segmentation, four weeks of organization, four weeks of acquisition. The teams we coached were almost uniformly ready to be coached. They had any number of problems—chaotic offices, angry clients, plateaued production, on and on—but they were willing to show up and willing to change. And for the first two coaching phases, they usually did.

Financial Advisor teams with books that were bloated with accounts that had been haphazardly accumulated or were not governed by a minimum number of assets or a maximum number of households took to Supernova segmentation like a drowning man grabbing a lifeline. Supernova was, in many ways, saving their professional lives. Teams that operated like an emergency room on a full-moon Saturday night knew they needed a bullet-proof organizational system, and Supernova took them through every step. Some teams were so ready they grasped the logic behind the program and ran ahead excitedly. Nearly every team we coached embraced Supernova's segmentation and organization practices regardless of what ailed them. However, when it came to setting the stage for acquisition the results from many teams were disappointing.

Team after team, year after year, went into acquisition with a lot of momentum and a lot of confidence. Team after team, year after year, essentially ignored the Supernova suite of acquisition tools, or failed to sustain an early commitment that actually delivered results.

The problem was sustainable growth. We were able to get a big lift by giving better service and getting organized. Other FAs were able to double their business. But, it wasn't sustainable.

There were often teams that already spent a good portion of their day in acquisition growing faster. It was the teams that hadn't been growing. Once they got their initial growth spurt from Supernova, they typically stalled out. They were delighted by Supernova, but we weren't. Try as we might, the formula for growth was not being adopted. We could see that these teams needed us to reinforce the process and keep them on the right track but they didn't seem to realize they had fallen off the wagon. Supernova moved on to new teams that needed us and we were sadly forced to leave those other teams behind.

Maybe a longer training program is the answer?

We went from three months of coaching to a one-year program. Sure, a longer program of three months of weekly coaching followed by once-a-month follow-up accountability sessions helped the teams focus more on growth. Still, the problem of keeping on track after coaching persisted.

The breakthrough came when we realized that we had the emphasis on the wrong syllable.

Wait, what?

It was baffling. It was maddening. It was throwing a dark shadow on of the extraordinary legacy of Supernova. If we couldn't consistently and repeatedly help our clients grow, maybe the legacy wasn't actually that extraordinary! Sobering stuff. I was truly baffled by the response I was getting. Until an extraordinary team engaged us. What this team presented to us awakened something in me I had been carrying for decades but had just stopped seeing in my day-to-day life. An extraordinary team proved something to me that I already believed in and had somehow forgotten the spirit living inside it.

It's all about giving.

Giving to give—not merely giving to get—is the key that unlocks everything. Personal satisfaction, professional accomplishment, income growth and passion; I'm going to tell you stories of teams that were hitting the ceiling. Now with Supernova coaching, they have broken through their barriers and are streaking higher in their production, enjoying elevated morale, increased client satisfaction levels, and improved quality of life. I'm going to walk you through what it takes to move your practice forward with Supernova while never letting go of this powerful human truth: to give is to experience joy.

It's also important to note that I'm not a social worker and neither are you. I'm not going to preach commercial abstinence or personal redemption. I'm simply going to show you what I've rediscovered about what I already knew and show you how to awaken it in your career—and your life.

These are big promises from a little book. But read on, and hang on, because everything could be changing soon, and I want you to enjoy the ride. I sure have.

Indulge me as I rewind the clock. It was 1994 and our team was winning. I was District Director for Merrill Lynch and my FA teams were embarrassing the other districts. Year after year, we brought back the top awards for gathering assets. The Masters, as it was called, was the program Merrill Lynch had in place to drive our FAs and their teams to increased production by increasing managed assets. I absolutely refused to lose. When I say I was embarrassing the other districts, I mean it literally. I heard some version of "So, what, you take pleasure in making us look bad?" many times. With a quiet smile I thought, "No, that's your issue." My issue is winning. This period of my management career is when I learned a lot about how to motivate and how to reward. I was laser focused on winning, and winning meant bringing in more new money than any other district. This is not to paint a picture of me as a work-obsessed take-no-prisoners boss. I was living a full life with a beautiful wife and two special children. You may see me as a singularly focused accomplishment machine. That might be closer to the truth. And then I got dinged.

"Rob, your production numbers are impressive as always, but your service scores stink. You're last in the entire organization."

OK, that wasn't a ding; it was a gut punch, an enormous ego hit. And from that single sentence Supernova was born.

Customers Are Always Right

What hurt even more than being at the bottom of the list was knowing we deserved it. Clients were marking us down on surveys—or leaving Merrill altogether—because we were falling down on the basic aspect of good customer service: responsiveness. In survey after survey, they told us they didn't like how we handled their phone calls and their requests. We were so busy hunting new assets that we were ignoring our existing clients and their concerns. Without attention, when they shifted from complaining to leaving, we really didn't have an answer. They were getting lousy service but it was the best service we could offer them, not because we were inherently deficient in servicing our clients but because we had too many clients to begin with.

We were asset-gathering champs and gathering meant grabbing and holding everything and everyone. If only success was measured in the number of clients, we would have been succeeding. It wasn't. Client service involved delivering what we promised to everyone in our books; we were miserable failures. We had deluded ourselves into denying one of the eternal truths in business: 80% of our business comes from 20% of our clients. The 80/20 Rule, and indeed it is a rule, like gravity is a law. But we just kept shoving new money through the door with no real thought to how we were going to service the people attached to it. More was better until it wasn't. We were winners in raw numbers but were losing the battle with time. Time for the attention our clients believed they would get from us and certainly deserved.

Our FAs and our Client Associates (CAs) were stretched to their very limits by the never-ending torrent of obligations —everything became an emergency; real emergencies never elevated above the cacophony of the everyday. A client calling with a time-sensitive question or an immediate problem got tossed onto the big stack of urgent calls to return. When I said above we were miserable failures, I mean on every level. We were experiencing misery—in client contact with delayed responses, in our team's morale because they were tossing water overboard with Dixie cups as the boat sank. There wasn't enough time in a day to handle the workload. Instead of streamlined and efficient, there were log-jams and so much backup it was raining stress. Unfortunately, the burdens followed some home.

An FA lost her father to cancer, and blamed herself one minute and Merrill the next, all because she was too overwhelmed with work to help him in his final few months, even though they lived just minutes apart. She left the firm in tears of shame with teeth clenched in rage. Marriages were failing and health issues were escalating, but hey, we won The Masters again. And still the clients fired us, or fired off feedback filled with disappointment and indignation.

Our growing service failures coincided with the rise of many independent and boutique advisory firms. These firms offered a more holistic level of service, which included a whole lot more than, say, impressive returns on a large cap fund could overcome. Our investment model couldn't keep clients, and discounts weren't buying their loyalty for long, if at all. If we were committed to getting back on top—and you better believe I was—then we had to improve. We had to deliver not just better service, but exceptional service. Next question: How do you deliver exceptional service?

Planning and Contact

Exceptional service emanated from creating a financial plan and then following through on implementing it. This was an under-appreciated and underused step in client service. We sure weren't doing it with any consistency, and I don't think anyone at Merrill was. Who was? The independents were. They sold planning before they sold returns, and in doing so they were building a wall around their clients. A wall that made their clients feel secure and kept us on the outside. It wasn't just good business for the advisors, it was a good practice for their clients.

A client's defined financial plan determined the decisions about where to invest their money and their time. So, what was the solution to poor service—hiring an army of CFPs (Certified Financial Planners)? Even if we did (and we didn't) there was no model for turning a plan into a sequence of purposeful actions. We were losing clients because we didn't offer them a plan, but that wasn't the only reason clients were defecting.

As you read above, clients were not happy with how we handled their calls, and once again they were right to be angry. A question or a problem just went into the return-call vacuum and took too long to be addressed. Our FA/CA and client contact was inconsistent or worse. Often the calls were intrusive. Yes, we had migrated most of our clients to a fee model, but that didn't stop us from calling when we had something to pitch. It may well have been an offer of a timely opportunity or a product that was ideal for them, but the point is we were calling to sell them something, not to listen to them. I say all this now in retrospect as if the service issues were easy enough to diagnose. They were not. We didn't know how to fix our service deficiencies because we didn't know what good service was, so we started investigating.

What Makes Exceptional Client Service so Exceptional?

It's a question that seems easy enough to answer, right? After all, we've each experienced first-class service. We know it when we see it and when we don't. But how much do we really understand about the business models beneath the visible expressions of exceptional service? I don't know about you, but at that point in the mid-90s we knew virtually nothing about the core principles of creating an exceptional service experience. Sensing that this was the missing critical piece to our approach and future, I challenged some of my team to start from the question: What makes exceptional client service exceptional? and follow where it took them. With an allocated budget and their calendars cleared, they were on a mission to success. The answers and insights they brought back became the core of Supernova.

A truly exceptional client service experience shares these principles:

- Financial Planning—Clients want to be heard and understood by their financial advisor. They need to be seen and respected as individuals with unique situations. They want to know they are listened to regarding their ideas about what they want and require. To meet their expectations, we need to provide a custom financial plan for them. Clients want an advisor who will get and keep them on task.
- Regular Client Contact.
- Rapid Response to Problems.

That's it. Clients want quick and timely responses from us and regular contact. They don't want their calls to be sales calls. They want to know they are a priority. Rapid response and regular contact. Sounds simple enough, right? Well, of course, it was impossible to implement in the current situation. We couldn't respond to anything rapidly because we were already responding to everything like it was an emergency—there was no order and no system, just frantic scrambling and constantly shifting priorities. Additionally, we couldn't contact every client on our list on a regular basis because we averaged 640 clients/FA.

As we thought about our current state of chaos, and about how to integrate this newly realized information, some things were starting to become clear. One thing in particular: we had too many clients who were taking too much time and contributing too little to the production.

Today it's standard practice, but at the time it was practically heresy to consider a smaller book of only your best clients. But back then it was a new solution to enable us to provide clients with excellent service. We had no idea how to actually execute our insight, but we had found our way to the answer, and we couldn't just ignore it. The formula was starting to come together... in theory, with fewer clients, we could respond to problems quickly and we could contact them regularly, especially if we were implementing a financial plan that was pacing the conversations. In theory. In reality, we were staring at an empty whiteboard. No plans, no timelines, no nothing. What we did know was: clients were the key and we intended to keep winning in the firm's FA performance competitions. Since the challenges were inclusive of asset acquisition and predicated on meeting the client's expectations, winning now had to be inclusive of service. Fine, then we were going to create the ultimate client experience. In driving, BMW had cornered it. In hospitality the Ritz Carlton defined it. In financial services we were going to own it. With the missing piece identified and defined, the framework to accomplish an exceptional client experience was added to the FA tool belt. It worked.

We were winning again. What happened?

The story of Supernova's ascent is thoroughly documented in *The Supernova Advisor*, so right here I'll sum it up this way: it worked spectacularly well. Once implemented and running at maximum effectiveness in FA teams, we returned to our rightful spot on top in the various FA campaigns. And yet, some tension from the old order remained. Imagine this conversation:

"Rob, how do you do that Supernova thing?"
"Come here for a week and we'll teach you."
"No, just give me the recipe, or the software, or whatever. It
    looks pretty simple to us."
"It is simple, but it's not easy."
"You never share anything."

That's condensed, but not inaccurate. As we were winning, I was getting a reputation as a guy who wouldn't share the secrets of his success. True? I didn't think so, but perception is reality in a large organization, so what I thought didn't really mean much. The good news is what I thought was about to be completely rewired... I was about to experience a life-changing force that would shift my world forever. His name was Larry Wilson.

Larry was an author, consultant, and motivator, and a guru. (At least he became a guru to me.) I first met him after sending a few of my specialists to one of his courses. They came back on fire, so I had my management team take his workshop. We returned equally charged. And armed with two principles that have never lost their central position in my career and my life. I had a newly defined purpose. I was on a mission. When I left for Larry's workshop, competing and winning would have been how I identified my purpose and mission (if I could have come up with one). I loved competing and especially loved winning. Although winning to me was not a scorched earth mindset I took no delight in seeing others lose.

And while Supernova was completely transformational for both the advisor and the client, I still wasn't seeing it all with the kind of clarity that would soon would reveal itself through the lens of my purpose and my mission.

What was my new purpose and mission? Simply stated:

> My purpose is to release the human potential by choosing growth over fear and by so doing help others to do the same.

Mission statements are both fuel and fences. They focus ideas and concepts into manageable plans. My mission is to boldly go where no person has gone before and joyfully share the map. Simply, I wanted to embolden advisors to create the practice of their dreams. We became committed to sharing, giving, and helping. We became aware of the fact that true happiness comes from **giving** and **helping**, and that became our mission as it is today.

With those two powerful personal directives, everything else began to fall into place. I would share Supernova by helping teams implement it in a direct and active intervention: education and coaching. We put together a Supernova road show that did more than show—it put each district several steps forward in implementing Supernova on their own. The stories of these adventures in corporate transformation run through *The Supernova Advisor.*

But after we kicked it off with a big show, we left a powerful team of one Supernova ninja in place for a week to work with each team, specifically on segmentation and organization. One by one, the districts had us in and team by team, Supernova began to embed itself. They were heady days and I will never forget the energy they created in and around me, but none of it would have happened if I hadn't been animated by a purpose to release the human potential by choosing growth over fear and by so doing to help others to do the same, and a mission to boldly go where no person has gone before and joyfully share the map.

As the years unfolded and we grew the Supernova Consulting Group, my purpose and my vision had become so deeply ingrained that I was almost unaware of them. They became like oxygen—always present but rarely acknowledged. I retired from Merrill and moved to Boca Grande. One day I ran into Larry Wilson and he, along with my daughter Courtney, pushed me to write the first book based on my experiences at Merrill Lynch. After I had written the book people in the business came calling asking me questions and wondering if I could be their coach. I couldn't resist. It was what I loved to do and wanted to do—to make a difference in the industry that I loved.

What Worked and What Didn't

Let's spend a few minutes analyzing why Supernova works and why it doesn't. The most valuable commodity that financial advisors lack is time. I recently heard the head of a major Wall Street firm say that with technology the average FA can now handle 440 clients. If that is true, we have come full circle.

In 1994 the average FA had 650 clients and was overwrought. They were losing one client for every one they brought in. Supernova gave those FAs back their lives. When they went down to 100 clients, provided a financial plan, met with clients on a monthly basis, and gave clients rapid response to their issues, they stopped losing clients. **They had time to grow and they grew!**

You could have 440 clients if you chose to have more $250,000 clients that don't need service. That model of a big book of low-asset clients works, but only if the expectation includes low levels of service. For FAs who have clients with assets of one to 20 million dollars, financial planning, 12-4-2, and rapid response are must haves. The "440 model" would take us right back to 1994 when we were losing one client for every one added. No one wants to go back to those days.

Technology give us the ability to better serve the clients we have. Instead of 12-4-2 we are able to deliver closer to 48-4-2. For example, we contact the client to set up their monthly appointment, confirm that appointment by email with an enclosed agenda, make the call at the appointed time, and then send an executive summary. That's four times a month or 48 times annually. The clients are delighted and you have effectively used technology.

Financial advisors were able to grow because they got their books skinny. Some chose to keep growing, to become world-class FAs, and others didn't; some chose 640 (or 440) clients and chaos. So where is the growth coming from at most major firms?

The Private Wealth Advisors/Private Bankers!

What are these Private Wealth Advisors (PWA) doing that the others aren't?

First, they shrank to grow. The average PWA has 50 clients.

Second, they have a team.[1]

Third, they are experts in planning.

Fourth, they have high minimums and they raise these consistently.

Fifth, they have very high service standards (monthly Supernova contact or more).

Sixth, they have high standards of activity, which leads to growth, and they track that activity.

Seventh, they typically receive qualified introductions from their delighted clients, who become raving fans.

Eighth, they have a few well-positioned Centers of Influence who give them regular introductions.

Ninth, they are motivated. Motivations vary widely, but they can always tell you the "why."

This is what all of our best FAs do regardless of whether they have a PWA/PB (Private Banker) designation or not.

The answer to "how to grow" as an FA, a team, or a firm is on the following pages. It is simple but not easy. It requires leaders to be coaches. Firms need to hire coaches to teach their leaders how to coach. The answer is not going back to the more-is-better model. It is about correctly executing an exceptional client-centered experience combined with an innovative growth strategy.

In the introduction, you read about how the consistent failure of Supernova teams to grow in ways the model practically demands was incredibly frustrating and baffling. I was so focused on my work sharing the Supernova map I wasn't seeing that Supernova—in and of itself—was about sharing and giving. I thought I would do the sharing and the teams would simply do the growing. The key to growing is giving. But before we can give we must become as efficient as possible. How do we maximize our talents and time? Well, that's the next chapter.

Read on . . .

NOTE

1. We have a whole other book on the subject of team building: Curtis Brown and Rob Knapp. 2018. *Supernova Advisor Teams, A Pathway to Excellence.* New York: John Wiley & Sons, Inc.

2

Organize and Operate

Raising Our Productivity by Maximizing Our Efficiency

How do we maximize our talents and time in an environment where the financial services industry is struggling to grow? The economies of the major Mergers and Acquisitions (M&A) deals have all been realized. Buying smaller firms and recruiting quality talent has been expensive and those costs have stacked up higher than returns. In short, strategic growth opportunities for financial services firms are dwindling. Raising client fees is a non-starter in such brutally competitive times, so that leaves organic growth. And by "organic" I mean actual people working harder than ever to increase productivity. To which FAs have either said, "Oh really? You want even more hours from me?" or, "actually, I'm happy with my production right now thank you very much."

But what if there was a way to accelerate growth without dumping more on the FA? What if that accelerated growth was driven by delighted clients offering enthusiastic introductions as they handed over more and more of their assets? Supernova makes it possible because Supernova organizes everything.

If Supernova had a list of commandments, this would top the list: Organize granularly to serve spectacularly. On the client-facing side, precise organization creates space in your day—and in your mind—to serve your clients. Supernova organization brings a laser focus to the things that create value and propel growth, and pushes out the things that distract, diminish, and destroy your focus. As the book unfolds, we'll go more in-depth into how client-facing Supernova organizing

17

principles can be a multiplier, but in this chapter, we're going to look internally.

Five Star Model

Supernova's guidance on how teams should organize and operate has evolved, matured, and become more sophisticated as a direct result of my team and myself coaching advisors directly. The core structure has endured from my original model. Five stars define five essential aspects of team operation and five critical roles. The five stars of Supernova are:

1. Planning
2. Implementation
3. Brand Management (Service)
4. Marketing
5. Leadership.

The Five Star Model is client-centered; four out of five roles of the team are entirely focused on the client, including marketing. How? In a Supernova practice, marketing conversations are opportunities to uncover ways the advisor can help, not products the firm can sell. Helping clients can elevate Supernova FAs to higher purposes and more meaningful relationships, which is also where assets collect, and networks enrich. And it all starts when you get organized. This is the client-centered practice.

The Language of Ownership

If you've been around Supernova in the past few years, you've seen us refer to the individuals responsible for each star as Vice Presidents (VP), as in the VP of Planning, VP of Brand, etc. If you like that, go with it. My coaches and I also heard that five "Vice Presidents" on an eight-person team felt too grandiose. I get it. Plenty of teams call the owners of each star a Director. That feels right for these pages, so that's what I'll use.

In this chapter and subsequent chapters, you'll learn more about the transformative potential contained in each star no matter how you define the owner and we will also explain the standards, strategies, goals, and follow up for each role.

The First Star: Director of Planning

An entire Supernova practice serves as the Chief Financial Officer (CFO) for their clients, and it's the Director of Planning who takes the lead. It's the responsibility of this role to make sure every single client gets an actual financial plan—one that envisions the next few years, few decades, and into the next generation. Naturally, this person is a Certified Financial Planner (CFP), but in a Supernova practice, every member should be well versed in the principles of planning.

I've seen teams in which every financial advisor had earned or was in the process of obtaining a CFP designation. That same office was growing steadily and under control as the clients saw the transformative effects of a plan that was implemented with discipline.

The Multigenerational Planning Process is not a book or a plan. Instead, it's an ongoing process that continually evolves in tune with the economy and particular client's needs. Many FAs struggle to decide whether or not to charge for planning. I suggest that both the FA and the client would take the financial planning stage and especially the implementation of that planning process more seriously if there was a professional fee.

Laurie Barry, a Supernova advocate and a serious financial planner, has decided to charge for planning. "For new clients, I tell them: 'Now we're charging for new planning up front.' I won't take on a new client unless they can pay a fee of $3,500–5,000. I let them know we're not taking on new clients. If they came from a referral of a client who didn't pay that fee, I explain our situation has changed. We're working with a limited number of clients, and we want to make sure that clients are engaged in the process. We also put a lot of time in the comprehensive analysis."

"We charge a planning fee regardless of the asset picture. We've been working on 2nd generation. I feel like a lot have been coming to us. We're getting some small accounts. Some of our second generations even pay a fee. A regular referral pays a fee. I feel like I don't have enough time so I'm charging for my time. However, I am strongly considering charging a fee to existing clients, kind of re-structuring how they pay us. I feel it's two separate services."

For Your Consideration

Do I charge for planning?

Would I do more planning if I did?

Would my clients take a financial plan I developed for them more seriously if they were charged for it?

The Second Star: Director of Implementation

If the Director of Planning is the doctor, the Director of Implementation is the pharmacist. They make sure the client's plan is executed and—as unpleasant as it can sometimes be—that the patient/client takes their medicine.

Implementation is a significant role in a healthy Supernova practice. This person is responsible for developing and delivering the client's Supernova investment strategy, which begins with risk tolerance but doesn't end there. Risk tolerance is a feeling. SMART planning works from more than feelings and opinions; it makes the age of the client the center of the plan. Every stage in life has financial challenges and opportunities that exist independent of risk tolerance. First, a Supernova advisor incorporates SMART planning to make sure the strategy is in perfect sync with the client's stage of life (see Figure 2.1). Second, the Director of Implementation "Supernovas" the investment process. And finally, the Director of Implementation also drives the office's 24-month calendar. This is an organized set of conversations that happen at set times with every client. In the next chapter, we will look at topics and the effectiveness of using them.

S	• Specific
M	• Measurable
A	• Attainable
R	• Results-focused
T	• Time-bound

Figure 2.1 Smart Marketing

The Third Star: Director of Brand Management

The term "brand" has been in the broader business culture for a while now, and with all the talk about how businesses invest in their brand and protect their brand, I believe there's still a lot of fuzziness about how to define a brand, especially in a service-oriented business like ours.

Here is a new thought for you: your brand is not determined by your best client, but by your worst!

Let's deconstruct that.

Your clients define your brand. It's their experiences that create your position in the market. Clients build or diminish your reputation. Clients succeed or don't with your guidance. Your firm's market position, your competition, and your logo all matter much less than how your clients define you.

Supernova makes every client an A client, but of course, they are not all the same. Their situations are different, and their personalities are unique. When it comes to your brand, your clients' perceptions of your service and their portfolio performance are more important than the reality. Perception is the reality, especially in the context of prospective clients. When they hear a negative comment or review—even a minor one—it is unlikely they have other information to counter that perception. It's critical that as you look to strengthen your brand (and it can always be reinforced) you look at how your worst client perceives you. Who is worse? It could be the complainer, or the chronically absent from your 12-4-2 sessions, or the one who just refuses to implement the financial plan.

Even if those clients do value you and understand that every issue is their issue, they are still your worst. You are falling short in your promise to guide their financial lives This should activate a candid exploration of what can be done so that they utilize what you are offering them, resulting in bringing them to a better place—better served, more engaged, committed to the plan, or reassigned to someone more suitable. All of that falls to the Director of Brand Management.

The person is part warrior and part steward. They protect several domains:

- Monitoring segmentation: Director of Brand owns the annual review of the book in which you set your minimum number of assets and maximum number of clients; they guide the conversation with questions like: Who comprises the 20% of our clients who are responsible for 80% of our production? What clients can we transition to another team so we can increase our minimum asset level? The Director of Brand Management is responsible for holding the line on segmentation. This is not always easy, but it is essential to Supernova growth.
- Rapid Response: It's woven deeply into your brand to respond quickly to client questions or issues. The Supernova standard is to contact them within an hour if the call comes in during business hours, and give them a resolution within 24 hours, or a clear communication as to when it will be resolved. It's the Director of Brand who makes sure the office has the right people and the right systems to deliver.
- 12-4-2: The Director of Brand makes sure the contact ritual is adhered to by both the clients and the financial advisors.
- Accountability for additions to the team meeting schedule board and scoreboard.
- Compliance: Supernova is compliance brought to life. In a high-functioning Supernova practice, good compliance behaviors are not some further obligation or unwieldy block to productivity; they are merely how Supernova

operates. Post-call/meeting notes go straight to the client folder or the Customer Relationship Manager (CRM). This is part of your brand too, and the Director owns it.

The Fourth Star: Director of Growth (Marketing)

Now we enter the direct realm for the Supernova multipliers. These tools, rituals, and processes are the authentic game changers in a Supernova practice. Show me a Supernova team that has hit a plateau, and I'll show you a team that is under-utilizing (or ignoring) one or more of the Supernova client acquisition strategies. The Director of Growth is the person responsible for holding the team accountable for embracing and implementing the Supernova acquisition strategies. The rest of this book is a deep dive into each of these Supernova multipliers. An abbreviated way to remember this approach is using the phrase: "90-6-4-2-2-1+1."

- 90-Day Free Look: For qualified clients who can't make a decision, offer a 90-day "free look." These prospects will receive an abbreviated plan (which allows you the opportunity to qualify them further), three months of 12-4-2, rapid response to issues, and planning if possible. This will give the prospect all the reasons they need to exit their existing FA relationship. This the traditional "puppy dog" close. Try taking an adorable puppy home for 90 days and then give it back at the end of the trial. Probably not going to happen!
- Six Centers of Influence: Centers of Influence (COIs) are people willing to introduce you to prospects on a regular basis without being asked. You will meet with these people regularly (ideally monthly) and explore how you can help them. This is reciprocity brought to life, and there is so much more to explore about the multiplying power of your COIs.
- A four-person Mastermind Group: This is a carefully curated set of people from other fields who are com-mitted to helping group members grow professionally

and personally. Introductions happen here, sure, but the larger purpose is to plug into the collected wisdom of the group and let it elevate you.

- Two Community Board positions: These are both passionate and strategic. Find organizations and causes that bring you to life and make you think strategically about the visibility that each board gives your practice. I recommend moving through the committee structure by eventually assuming critical positions in development, executive leadership, and ultimately the presidency. And think in five-year cycles—from first meeting to the presidency in five years, then leaving after your term has ended. This keeps the board fresh and will position you for your next high-visibility board and all the right things that happen because of it.

- Two Niches: First, a natural niche "where you came from," and second, the target niche that reveals itself based on where you acquire clients. Maybe you already have several clients in top positions at a Fortune 500 company. That's a natural niche. A target niche might be a particular subset of professionals, doctors who are selling their practice, for example. There's a lot of multiplying power in this area, and we'll get more in-depth in the pages ahead.

- One Social Networking Plan: This is the active use of LinkedIn and Facebook to build your connections, reach out to your network with meaningful messaging and content, and create your platform, where thought leadership can grow post by post.

- One "ask" for an introduction from a client during each in-person meeting. Notice I don't call them "referrals." Getting referrals is a tired play in the sales handbook. All taking and no giving. That's not Supernova. Supernova practices grow on earning intentional and meaningful introductions, not a casually tossed off list of names. This gives your clients the opportunity to reciprocate and help their friends find the best financial advisor to help them invest their money.

If you totaled the power of these four stars, it wouldn't equal the multiplying power of the last star, Leadership. A Supernova practice grows when the leadership role is well defined, and the leader is prepared to serve. Let's talk about both.

The Fifth Star: Director of Leadership

Supernova is, first and foremost, a service model. Its organizing principles are all calibrated toward creating the ultimate client experience and then building a brand on the service you deliver. However, our definition of "service" doesn't reside exclusively with your clients; the leader of a Supernova team is also in the service business. They are in that role precisely to serve everyone else on the team:

- Supernova leaders create an environment that allows people to grow (and occasionally fail).
- Supernova leaders work to remove or minimize barriers to team member productivity.
- Supernova leaders establish the metrics of success and then hold everyone—especially themselves— accountable. (If you haven't figured it out by now, Supernova leadership is modeled on the principles of servant leadership.)

As a human ideal, servant leadership has been around for a long time. The ideals formed a movement in 1970 with the release of the book by Robert K. Greenleaf, *The Servant as Leader*. It was the cultural debut of the terms "servant leader" and "servant leadership." Here's how he defined it: "The servant leader is servant first... It begins with the natural feeling that one wants to serve first. Then conscious choice brings one to aspire to lead. That person is sharply different from one who is the leader first."

You got that sequence, didn't you? The impulse to serve is what brings to life the call to lead. Too many teams/companies/ nations have been led in the wrong direction by leaders who saw themselves as "the leader" with no underlying foundation to serve and elevate. Back to Greenleaf: "The difference manifests itself in the care taken by the servant first to make sure that other people's highest priority needs are being served. The best test is: Do those served grow as persons? Do they, while being served, become healthier, wiser, freer, more autonomous, more likely themselves to become servants?"

The servant leader is the servant first, which is not anywhere close to being servile; it is about wanting to help others. It is about identifying and meeting the needs of colleagues, clients, and communities. And while we're on the subject of what defines a Supernova leader, let's be clear about what they are not:

- A leader on a Supernova team is not necessarily the highest producer.
- A leader on a Supernova team is not necessarily the most visible in the community.
- And a leader on a Supernova team is probably not the loudest voice or the largest ego.

As you explore the rest of the book, you'll encounter specific examples of what a Supernova leader looks like in practice and what they can accomplish in the lives of the team and the clients. As Larry Wilson was fond of saying, "Managers get work done through people; servant leaders get people done through work."

The Leader's Role

As you'll see, every role in a Supernova practice is highly specialized with very specific responsibilities. Focus and productivity are accelerated when you first define the roles, and then keep everyone on their own path. Sounds complicated and limiting? Give it a shot anyway. You'll find plenty of opportunities to offer opinions in areas outside your role. By assigning responsibility and expecting accountability, Supernova narrows the field of view and—perhaps paradoxically—expands the possibilities. That said, the leader's role has probably the least specificity.

Remember, a Supernova leader is a servant leader, and that service begins with these questions:

- What is on your mind?
- What do you need from me, and the rest of this team, to deliver on your commitments to us?
- What is slowing your progress and what could you accomplish if it wasn't there?
- When you worry about work, and about life, what occupies your thoughts?
- When you imagine what your career can become, what are you seeing?
- How am I doing as a leader?
- What are the most impactful takeaways from our conversation today?

Supernova leaders ask these questions and more, and they ask them repeatedly. The answers shape what the leader does, and everything the leader does needs to help team members access and release their potential by choosing growth over fear. For some it's a more comfortable choice than for others. Knowing where each person is within that arc is the art of Supernova leadership.

Fortunately, there are also tools we offer to help you.

- 12-4-2 everyone. This is the contact ritual for clients. Supernova FAs schedule a set time for 12 monthly calls, four portfolio reviews with two of those in person. It's also the model for organizing the dialogue between a Supernova leader and everyone on the team. I've seen it sliced several ways:
- Two lunches outside the office to allow for more personal conversations.
- Two review sessions where the leader helps rework the direction of a business plan for a team or individual FA.

- 12 monthly 45-minute sessions with an agenda and executive summary.
- Team meetings: Every morning there's a quick stand-up that sets the day in motion with upcoming meetings and important calls. Every Monday, the full team talks marketing with the **Gameboard (Giving Board)**. Who is meeting with whom? Who is connecting people and why? Where are we against our growth metrics? Every Thursday, each Director reports to the full group: here's what we said we were going to do, here's what we accomplished, here's what we're committing to in the week ahead. Those results all go on the **Scoreboard**, which is mostly a public statement of commitment and accountability made visible. These meetings are locked on the calendar and shifted only when there's no other way, major holidays, major earthquake, but that's about it. No calls scheduled here, no excuses. Everyone shows up, and everyone has a voice.
- The Business Plan: Supernova leaders have a ready-made template for detailing where the group is going: the five stars. Leverage that structure and the commitments of each Director to construct a plan. New clients acquired (and existing clients handed off to make room for them). Net new money. Production. CFP designations earned. Niches defined and inhabited. Mastermind groups formed or joined. Board seats occupied. Everything that each Director owns is the raw material for the business plan, and the leader owns that.
- The foundation and the messages: What are your purpose and mission as a group? And how do you explain what you do in your 15-minute elevator speech or your value proposition? Those are big questions that don't fall exclusively to the leader, but the leader does guide the team through the sessions where they are explored and ultimately determined.

A Supernova Director of Leadership has a big job. They ask big questions and are responsible for wrapping themselves around them. A Supernova leader must elevate team confidence, expand team capabilities, and monitor individual accountability. It's part counselor, part visionary, and zero part ego. Service guides every decision and every action.

Why is the Supernova multiplier so important?

Financial service companies are still organized like it's 1970 and everything is about making the sale. A President and a National Sales Director are at the top of the hierarchy, and it is a hierarchy that is hard to change or avoid. Sure, there are departments and divisions charged with financial planning, product development, operations, and even service. But sales runs the show, and that has created a massive disconnect between the firm and the client. Today, we are in the client service business. We are financial consultants with a fiduciary standard no matter what regulations mandate, or don't. We owe our clients exceptional service, and for the most part, we're failing.

As an industry, we don't consistently measure client satisfaction, or incentivize outstanding service beyond a plaque at a ceremony. At the corporate policy level, we're not naturally organized to serve. Imagine the firm that changes all that. It would disrupt the industry in the same way that Amazon, Southwest, or Disney did theirs. Focusing on client needs above all else transforms corporate cultures. And it will take an obsessive mindset because the institutional barriers are enormous. But the upside is even more significant. The firm that puts the client at the center of the organization—not just on a slide for the executive committee, but truly at the center of organizational priorities—will own the future. Everyone else will be playing catch up. So, who wants it?

Radical Delegation and What My Dad Said

If we're lucky enough to be well-parented (and I was), we'll often enter adulthood carrying great gifts. We may or may not be consciously aware of them. We may not realize their greatness until much later. When you are subject to optimal parenting there are all manner of useful gifts and lessons deposited into our psyches. The power of a negative example can provide a purpose that drives one toward a remarkable life. In my case my father was a positive example. With a single sentence I'll never forget, he armed me with an idea that grew more and more powerful the longer I carried it forward.

My father was an industrial engineer for Armstrong. The company made linoleum floors, and his job was to make them more efficiently. He was given the task of relentlessly squeezing costs out of the manufacturing process; and relentless he was. He used to say, "believing you've eliminated all the costs was just a failure of imagination."

Dad was a smart guy, and even my 15-year-old self wanted to learn something from him. I asked him one Saturday when he brought me into the office, "What's your job?" His answer is the gift he gave me. He said, "My job is to eliminate my job—my job is getting everyone else to do the stuff that's in the job description so that I can think up new things."

His job was to think, to envision cost savings, to invent new workflows. It wasn't to send memos or sit in staff meetings (although I'm sure he did his share of each). And with that idea perking inside me, I entered adulthood. As my career unfolded and Supernova emerged, the idea of getting other people to do your job so you can do your real job crystallized into a bedrock principle I live by. Today, I call it radical delegation.

It's easy to see this principle at work in a growing Supernova practice. The administrator runs the office. They schedule the 12-4-2 sessions; they move the folders into place, they even schedule the acquisition calls. Why? First off, they are organized and dispassionate about the tasks, meaning they are more resistant to avoidance and procrastination. But most importantly, it's not your job.

Your job as a leader and FA is to think about your clients and your team. Your job is to get deeper and deeper into their lives so that you can understand the complexity and respond with a plan and with solutions that make their lives better. Your job is to become your client's CFO, and as soon as you think you've done everything you can you have what Pop would call "a failure of imagination."

Cultural Building Blocks

The day-to-day operational advantages of radical delegation are evident to all who have mastered it. (And learning it is no easy feat.) But I want to broaden the lens and look at delegation as an integral aspect of building a culture capable of sustaining success by creating breakthrough change. (It all was made clear to me at the moment some might define as failure—or at least as a step backward. I call it one of the great successes of my career).

I was a District Director for Merrill Lynch. I was responsible for the performance of 2,000 advisors in 14 states. It was a big job, and yet I insisted on doing it in a small way. Instead of sitting in my office broadcasting emails and jumping on and off calls, I got on a plane. My idea of leading is face to face. It's the best way to hear what's happening and the only way to elevate performance that lasts longer than the latest production ranking. It also meant that if I had any hope of remaining sane, I needed to practice radical delegation. That meant a phenomenal administrative team, which I had.

I learned early on to abandon any status that came with a primo office and to cram into any space that put me close to my administrative support. They were going to do a lot for me. I didn't want to have to shout down the hall. But there's another kind of delegation that defined my tenure running the district, and that's the real lesson.

I had a handful of direct reports—service, sales, and administrative managers who worked with me across the district—as well as complex managers who ran individual states. There's a lot to say about how I hired those people and the kind of leaders they became once they were leading with Supernova, but that's another chapter. What you need to know is that each of these people didn't just report to me, they also did big parts of my job, at least as detailed in the job description.

Classic example: two FAs in dispute over an account insist on "elevating it to the district." Essentially, they want me to referee, and I always said no. "You may see it as my job, and the job description may suggest it, but it's not the case," I said.

I believe the complex manager knows the dynamic much better and—if we hired right—has the wisdom to make the call and live with the fallout. The rare occasion on which a manager brought me an FA dispute, I would simply say, "I am happy to step in and handle this dispute, but then why do I have you?" That always solved the problem for me and if it didn't I had to ask if we had the right person in that role.

My Supernova hiring and management philosophy is simple: hire good people, delegate, and hold them accountable. But like so many things related to Supernova that isn't an easy thing to do. I think people resist delegating for three essential reasons—psychological, organizational, and technical—but they all share a single root: fear. Your Supernova journey is, at its core, about facing fear and growing as a professional and as a person.

Psychological Resistance

This is pure fear, disguised as rational thought. This is a fear of being seen as less than (fill in the blank). Fill in the blank with your peers, your boss, your staff, the persona you've created for yourself. Whatever, it's all ego—and your ego fights against fear like a wounded animal in a corner. The only way I know to be effective in the face of fear like this is to break it down. Look at your big to-do list and ask yourself: "In which of the tasks/responsibilities am I the only person in my organization with the knowledge, skills, and expertise to do it successfully?" You'll choose a few and be a warrior for those. You'll also find plenty of assignments other people can do just as well as you can. Every time you successfully delegate an assignment to someone else you are putting your fear back in the box where it belongs. Just the exercise alone can go a long way toward putting fear back in the box.

Organizational Resistance

I get it. Most teams are stretched thin, and asking you delegate gets a "Delegate? Ya right . . . " OK, time to get creative. Find an intern. Hire a temp. Identify a virtual assistant. Share a function with another team. And never stop asking if you're doing something because you've always done it, or because it directly improves the client experience. Southwest Airlines has a powerful goal—to be the nation's leading low-cost airline—and every decision they make runs through that filter, from the snacks they serve to the fuel contracts they enter. "Will it help us be the nation's leading low-cost airline?" If the answer is no, they don't do it.

Technical Resistance

This is about skills and practice. We've all—myself included—failed when delegating in the past. The work was wrong or late, or the act of delegating was so tortured and time-consuming that the only reasonable response was "I could have had it done by now." Don't go there. Don't blame the practice of delegation, practice being a better delegator.

- Be clear on the goal, but don't lay out every step to get there. Paint a clear picture of success, but if you dictate the process in minute detail, you'll not only devour your time you'll also de-motivate and dampen creativity. That's called micro-managing, not leading.
- Examine and critique your assumptions. If delegation is going to succeed, the most significant barrier to overcome may be your beliefs. What assumptions are you making about the skills and knowledge of the person you're delegating to? Do they understand the goals or do you assume they do? Check your assumptions against reality with brutal honesty, and then move to fill the gaps.
- Always be listening. Always be teaching. The day of the deadline is the worst time to see outcomes for the first time. Effective delegation is not an isolation chamber; it's an ongoing conversation. Regular updates and casual check-ins can identify approaching roadblocks well before they block progress. Feedback and suggestions are the prices of delegation.

Radical Delegation in Action

I was recently coaching a team in Columbia, South Carolina, who have been engaged in the Supernova Coaching process for about one year. Like many teams they were struggling with a busy travel schedule for the senior member of the team. They had to reschedule too many client meetings, and it was frustrating for the Client Service Associate (CSA). After several questions, they decided to keep the 12-4-2 phone appointments but reschedule the in-person meetings if the senior FA was pulled away due to travel. They also committed to better long-term planning so there would be fewer last-minute changes. Radical delegation doesn't have to be drastic. You must believe your team is capable of taking over when you are out. The military is built on the concept of cross-training in anticipation of taking casualties. This should be your model also.

Now I want you to consider using Operation Pushdown—this is a multiplier! This is how you create time. Do this each year then do it again. What is it? Once a year write down every responsibility or task that needs to be accomplished to make the team run smoothly.

First list the roles and responsibilities that you have to do that no one else can do, and then list the duties that someone else could do. Then debate who would be the best person to do that duty. Everyone is going to be delegating, so everyone is going to free up some time. Now since everyone is delegating, what's left at the bottom? Before you hire someone, determine if there is anything that is expendable. Decide what is sacred and what isn't. Financial planning, rapid response, and 12-4-2 are sacred. Everything else is on the table.

For example: Are you mailing out a marketing letter? That's one of those nice things, but not critical. Examine everything to determine what is crucial without cutting what is sacred.

Here is another example: You may like doing transactional business managing portfolios of individual stocks; however, if you moved to managing money on a discretionary basis, you can cut 50% of your time—and your performance could improve. What is 50% of your time worth? With discretionary investing, you're focused on the client's best interest, the client is getting more value, and you'll probably give yourself a pay increase. You eliminate the conflict of interest and the idea that you talk to clients only when you buy and sell. When you take three weeks to buy or sell a position because you've got every client in it and you've got to reach out to all of them, several may be disadvantaged due to the time delay. Finally, you will spend less time with your compliance department when you eliminate transactional business. Managing portfolios can give you some real cash, just do it in a discretionary way.

Keeping small accounts is another place to rethink your strategy. It's not in your clients' or your team's best interests to hide these accounts under the rug or in the closet. In reality, it wastes your time and your assistant's time. You may be keeping them because of sentimentality, or you think you're doing them a favor. In reality, you're typically ignoring them and not reviewing their account on a regular basis. They would be better served by a smaller, newer team who would appreciate them and spend more time focusing on their relationship.

Radical delegation, when completed, doesn't appear to be very radical at all. Instead, it is very logical. Not only does it free up valuable time but it transforms team members into extremely efficient, client-centered machines. You've created a Supernova multiplier.

CHALLENGE

Organize your team around the Five Star Model by delineating roles and responsibilities.

- Write a one-page business plan for each role with one-, three-, and five-year goals.
- Work the one-year plan backward into monthly goals and weekly goals.
- Have a Thursday afternoon meeting where you ask each Director to report on their progress versus goals. Use our format (Five Star Model) to present your team to COIs and more substantial prospects.
- And then launch Operation Pushdown. Practice cross-training and adopt the "Logical Delegation" model.

CHAPTER

3

Giving More and Keeping Score

Something wasn't working with the Supernova Gameboard™, and I've finally figured it out. But first let me give you the background behind this concept. The Supernova Gameboard™ emerged as a leadership tool when Supernova morphed into a comprehensive, cohesive model. Its core purpose is to measure activities—not results—and once implemented, it redistributes leadership across the practice by activating a powerful human behavior: accountability.

A Simple Dental Practice Inspired Me

The Supernova Gameboard™ had its roots in a dental practice, but not just any dental practice. A consulting group that evaluates profitability of dental businesses named this business "the most productive dental practice in the nation." The dentist driving it also happened to be the father-in-law of Darby Henley, a former sales manager of mine.

The Gameboard™ was a poster that listed everyone in the dental practice and their quantifiable tasked goals for the week. When each person hit their goal, or exceeded it, they wrote the number in black on the white board. If the person who did the scheduling didn't hit the goal, the realized number was written in red. Right there, for all to see, was a transparent view of the collective activities of each member of the practice. The board didn't collect the results of the activities. It captured the actions that, when practiced with discipline, created results. That's an essential understanding of success: Activities Create Results.

When a practice can see actions measured against goals, accountability reigns and ambiguity evaporates. Consistently hitting or exceeding a goal is a clear sign of increasing efficiency and productivity that signals to the leader that the team member is ready to reach a higher goal. Conversely, consistently missed goals are a sign that the individual needs assistance. Help comes by way of evaluating whether the missed goals are an indicator that the target is out of line with either the person's role or their abilities. This assessment would consequently lead to a change in the staff member's original job responsibilities or replacement of the person in that position. The Gameboard™ made individual commitments and goals visible to the entire team. I marveled at how high-functioning practices could use the Gameboard™ to identify opportunities to help one another and to hold each other accountable. I coached it to teams—heck, I preached it.

But instead of hearing "amen!" I mostly heard "meh."

There is no more underutilized tool in the Supernova toolkit than the Gameboard. I noticed the financial advisors I worked with over the years weren't integrating it into their practice or, even worse, they tried to use it and then dropped it. I realized it wasn't resonating with the teams we coached.

As I was discussing this with the advisors I was coaching two things came to light: the unrecognized power of giving, and the universal appeal of keeping score. I realized this was the missing piece. Let's look at each of these forces individually and then bring them together in the day-to-day life of a Supernova practice.

The Rule that Rules Us

The rule of reciprocity may fall short of a verified law of nature, but it's nearly as immutable. The rule of reciprocity holds that when we have received something of value, we are motivated to return the favor. Call it simple human civility. And when you deploy reciprocity with true generosity, it also can drive the growth of a Supernova practice.

In fact, it is the only driver of growth that is consistent and controllable.

You cannot control how much you get, but you can control how much you give. Sure, you can have an associate work all day on cold calls and occasionally land a decent client (as in lightning sometimes strikes, too). Or you can move your production north by riding the market when it's moving the right way. You, and every other advisor. But think about any other moment of growth, and I'll show you the rule of reciprocity at work.

A business owner approaching a big liquidity event gets your name from a business associate and calls you. (You got the introduction because you gave something of value to that associate.)

A prospect arrives in your office because she's heard your team just doesn't let anything slip. (She's there because you gave her neighbor Ritz-Carlton level service that caused her to sing your praises.)

A new client brings you their substantial wealth and their considerable mess. They've heard you will implement a client's plan with the same level of detail and determination that other advisors demonstrate in chasing new business.

An advisor with a fabulous book of business plans to retire and moves it all to you. He sees how your leadership stewards a high-performance culture that values professional development as much as professional accomplishment. You invested in yourself and your team, and now it is returning unexpected dividends.

Draw a line backward from each real win, and you will find it ends with a practice of giving. You gave high-quality, well-considered referrals. You insisted on a detailed financial plan (a valuable gift, regardless of the price tag) and you devoted resources to implement it, which added zero to your production but enormously to your brand. You elevated your profile on LinkedIn by posting original thought pieces, making meaningful connections, and acknowledging the successes of the people in your network—even those who you hardly know, but who you genuinely celebrate. It's all a gift, and it all ignites reciprocity. It may not lead to anything today or tomorrow, but it will lead to amazing things IF you do it consistently and with a mindset that's calibrated more to long-term than short-term payback. We give to give, then we get.

All of this made a huge amount of sense to me. I now know I was missing a more significant opportunity than just measuring activities to generate results. By tying it to a light-hearted activity (a game), I minimized its true essence, which has nothing to do with play and everything to do with growth. More specifically, the growth that naturally follows the critical Supernova mindset of "giving to get." So we decided to toss the Gameboard from the Supernova toolkit and create the Giving Board.

There it was. The Gameboard became the Giving Board, and within the time I've been coaching it, I've seen teams deeply accelerate their growth when they integrated this tool. A gentle reminder for the thousandth time, Supernova is about growth. And how can you be sure you're growing? You keep score.

What can go wrong when you are a true giver? Giving to a taker like Bernie Madoff wouldn't work. Be sure you are giving to a COI who is a giver or at least a matcher.

It's Monday—Time to Claim What You're Giving

In a high-performing Supernova practice, the Giving Board takes center stage in the team's meeting, but it's not really about the team today. It's about every person on the team, and what they are committed to giving. That includes giving to their clients, their Centers of Influence, and the rest of the team. At this point, the Rule of Reciprocity takes its first steps. Take a look at what each FA is committed to giving in Table 3.1.

Table 3.1   Financial Advisors' Giving Board Template

FA Name	Prospect Meetings	Converted to 90 Day Trial	VIPSA	Client Meetings Held	# of Introductions Given	Mastermind Group/ COIs/ Board Meetings Status[a]	Niche Activity
	Goal/ Actual	Goal/ Actual	Goal/ Actual	Goal/ Actual	Goal/ Actual	Goal/ Actual	
Rob							
George							
Mary							

[a]See "Measuring Activities"

Measuring Activities

For your Centers of Influence, Mastermind Group and civic/not-for-profit boards, giving will be measured by activities you accomplish.

For example, COIs would include:

- Giving the COI introductions to current clients looking for an Enthusiastically Endorsed professional such as an attorney or CPA
- Meeting with one of their clients who needs investing advice or a financial advisor
- Sharing your client-centered Supernova Process to help them.

Board Activity might include:

- Sponsoring a fundraiser
- Purchasing a table at an event
- Calling on potential donors
- Attending a board or committee meeting
- Meeting with fellow board members to explain your investment process.

Brand Activity might include:

- Attending board committee meetings
- Meeting with fellow board members to learn more about them and develop a friendship.

For Administrative Assistants or office staff, you would take their current role and measure it weekly. It would look something like Table 3.2.

There is tremendous power in these boards' simplicity because they form a rock-solid foundation from which each team can build. Some teams keep them just like this. Some teams modify them slightly, but the core principles remain. Measure commitments to activities that are designed to give more than is received.

Table 3.2 Administrative/Client Service Associates' Giving Board Template

Name	Betty		Marc		Laura	
	Goal	Actual	Goal	Actual	Goal	Actual
Appts. Made						
Appts. Confirmed						
Agenda Sent						
Folders Updated						
Notes Transcribed						
Exe. Sum. Set						
Rapid Response						
12-4-2 Appts. Added to Calendar						

It's Friday (or Thursday)—Time to Total Everything Up with the Scoreboard

Monday's meeting begins the week using the Giving Board and it wraps up on Friday with all eyes on the Scoreboard. This is where the Five Stars of Supernova form the core organizing principle. Each director is responsible for collecting the results from the giving activity in their area of responsibility and then reporting to the full team aggregated totals for their star. We defined the roles of the Five Stars in the last chapter. Here is our deeper dive into what each of them is expected to accomplish.

It's clear that advisors and advisory teams are results-oriented creatures. There's something encoded in their genes that drives them to measure themselves against, well, everyone . . . their past performance, their peers' performance, their competitors' performance. Some of it is the way markets and market-thinking imprint themselves on the brain. But facts are facts. FAs like to know the score.

And why not? Watch an NBA point guard bring the ball up court. You'll probably see him glance at the Scoreboard and ask himself "What is the score and how much time is left in this period?" In any high-scoring sport where the numbers accumulate quickly, there's a constant hunger to know the score. It helps determine strategy and calibrate effort. It is a time to think defensively and protect a lead or amp up the energy to rally. And since every FA is asking themselves some version of those questions anyway, let's reframe them and capture the answers in a tool that fits perfectly in the Supernova suite of tools.

The Scoreboard is built on the same principle as the Giving Board: activities generate results. But the Scoreboard goes beyond a production number, or rather, goes underneath the production number to measure and score the incremental wins that add up to a production total. The Scoreboard aggregates the giving activities that individuals committed to on the Giving Board, and reports the collective misses and the collective successes back to the entire team. Let's move it all from the abstract to the concrete: see Table 3.3.

The Director of Planning reports on the number of plans completed and is responsible for making sure every client has a plan. They act as a forensic scientist tasked with understanding what the client wants, not just what the client says they want. If every member of the team does their planning, they will also monitor the progress, so there is 100% compliance with the plan. If a team member is working toward a CFP designation that status is also reported.

The Director of Planning sets standards, strategies, goals, and follow-up guidelines for the team.

- **Standards:** We offer high-quality planning and we offer every client insurance products; mortgage financing; asset, liability and risk management; and estate and philanthropic planning.
- **Strategy:** Our planning is comprehensive therefore we charge for it. Question to consider: Do we offer the same plan based on risk tolerance or different plans for different circumstances?
- **Goals:** Every client has a plan and the plan is reviewed annually. We manage our clients' risks concerning taxes, legal, and litigation. Every client has a risk analysis, tax analysis, historical analyses, and adherence to plan execution.

Table 3.3   Supernova Scoreboard

Assigned Role	Activities	Short-Term Goals	Long-Term Goals	Follow Up
Director of Planning	Update on planning for all clients (any issues), other products being offered	Schedule planning meeting with three new clients	Every client has a plan in place, and was offered long-term-care insurance	Yes
Director of Implementation	Update on monthly client topics, updated plans, and their execution	Topics created and script written. All plans are under review annually	Update topics every two years, planning reviewed and updated as needed	
Director of Brand Management	Update on scheduling, folders, client concerns, compliance issues	Call two clients to reschedule in-person meeting, send executive summary to clients we met with this week	Folders completed for every client, 12-4-2 runs smoothly	
Director of Marketing	Update on 90-6-4-2-2-1 strategies	Review LinkedIn page, create team brochure, have new photo taken of team	All strategies are fully implemented and updated as needed	
Director of Leadership	Update on new assets, production goals, liabilities	12-4-2 the team, recruit new CSA, plan client event	Team is working efficiently, every FA has 50+ clients with a hard min/max	

- **Follow Up:** We use a (Gameboard) Giving Board to follow up on planning at our weekly team meeting.

The Director of Implementation is the boss of the 24-month calendar (Table 3.4). This is the template for your monthly calls. We recommend eight topics spread over two years, with a deep dive into each as appropriate. I suggest you choose from

Table 3.4 24-month calendar

Month	Year 1	Year 2
Jan	Full-Year Outlook	Full-Year Outlook
Feb	Annuity Review	Disability
Mar	Annuity Review Follow Up	Disability Follow Up
Apr	IRA Contribution, Roth, Tax Questions	Tax-Free Muni Review, Outlook
May	Long-Term Care	Tax-Free Muni Follow Up
June	Mid-Year Outlook	529 Intro Children/ Grandchildren, Mid-Year Outlook
July	Life Insurance Review	529 Follow Up
Aug	Life Insurance Follow Up	Estate Planning Trust
Sept	Mortgages	Estate Planning Trust Follow Up
Oct	Required Min. Distrib. (RMD)	RMD
Nov	Tax Selling, Harvesting, RMD	RMD, Tax Selling
Dec	Balancing Gains/Losses, Rebalancing Portfolios	Tax Selling, Rebalancing Portfolios

these topics: estate planning, mortgages, life insurance, annuities, long-term care, IRA (Individual Retirement Account) contributions, required minimum distributions (RMDs), disability, tax harvesting, tax-free municipal bonds (munis), and end-of-life planning. You set the topics, and every client is brought into the conversation at roughly the same time. This allows your team to focus on a particular topic and be better prepared and equipped for those conversations and subsequent questions as they have sharpened and updated their knowledge for one topic instead of all eight. It's also an opportune time to talk with your clients about the other professionals who advise them, to measure the client's enthusiasm for each, and to enlarge your network of professionals whom you can help and who will eventually help you. Ask clients who their other service providers (physicians, accountants, etc.) are and if they would enthusiastically endorse them. This feedback can be turned into a list of professionals and added to your network of Centers of Influence and referrals for other clients needing their services. It could be long-term-care insurance or estate planning or debt strategy, but every month has a topic that each FA offers to explore with each client. Do you think there will be a productive conversation around each topic with each client? Of course not. But as each month ticks by, you will deepen your relevance to clients as an advisor who gives advice.

This role also includes the responsibility to "Supernova" the investment process. No longer are there 300 investment choices. Twenty percent of the choices gives you 80% of the results—so focus! This director runs a tight ship regarding who gets in and who is kicked out of the investment matrix. The investment process is as rigorous as the service process. You have to follow the process to the letter and avoid careless mistakes. Don't fall into the "Funds for Lunch" trap quid pro quo. Every new investment offering has to get through the same rigorous evaluation and screening process.

The Director of Implementation is the guiding voice on the team's adherence to a consistent process related to the invest-ment model and the liability strategies. Any updates on that process are reported at this session. This director sets standards, strategies, and goals for the team and then follows up on the set guidelines.

- **Standards:** To have a consistent asset-allocation model and investment matrix for all clients with no deviations from that matrix unless approved by the Director of Implementation and to implement everything determined critical by the financial planner.
- **Strategy:** Create a list of items from the financial plan that need to be implemented, check them off as they are com-pleted, and review periodically.
- **Goals:** To have a consistent allocation model and investment matrix that is fully implemented.
- **Follow Up:** Monitor performance and implementation. Make adjustments to the asset-allocation model and investment matrix as needed.

These eight topics are chosen by the Director of Implementation and last two months. All other topics are calendar driven and recur annually.

The Director of Brand Management is the steward (or the police officer) of your team's core organization. This role encompasses segmenting for growth, rapid response, and 12-4-2. It covers all the practices that your team can leverage in a conversation with a prospect. The Brand Management umbrella envelops activities that can be measured, both individually and collectively. Compliance belongs here and is reported here. Maintaining the Giving Board and Scoreboard, scheduling all meetings, responsibility for rapid response, and rescheduling meetings that are in conflict with the FAs' schedules are also key functions of this director.

Standards, strategies, and goals this director sets for the team and then tracks include:

- **Standards:** Proactive client service (12-4-2), segmenting as needed, rapid response and follow up to client contact for compliance.
- **Strategy:** Create your ideal day and schedule clients for monthly meetings accordingly. Return client phone calls within one hour during regular business hours and resolve their issues promptly. Annually review your min/max and segment as needed.
- **Goals:** Every client is scheduled for a static monthly appointment, inquiries are answered immediately, compliance regulations are met.
- **Follow Up:** Number of client appointments is measured using the Gameboard at the weekly team meeting.

The Director of Growth (Marketing) owns the most potent activities of growth (of course, every Supernova activity should

Table 3.5 Template for growth activities on a team

FA Assigned	Possible Introduction	Date of Contact	Qual- ified?	Proposal Pre- sented	Poten- tial Reve- nues	Commit Date	Actual Reve- nues
	1. 2. 3.	1. 2. 3.	1. 2. 3.	1. 2. 3.	1. 2. 3.	1. 2. 3.	1. 2. 3.
	1. 2.	1. 2.	1. 2.	1. 2.	1. 2.	1. 2.	1. 2.
	1. 2. 3.	1. 2. 3.	1. 2. 3.	1. 2. 3.	1. 2. 3.	1. 2. 3.	1. 2. 3.
Totals							

contribute to growth). At the Friday session, the Director of Growth reports on the aggregated contacts with COIs, Mastermind Group meetings and conversations that emerge, VIPSA conversations, LinkedIn activities, who is in the prospect pipeline, and more. If it directly connects to growth, the Director brings it to this session. Table 3.5 is a basic view of a sample pipeline. (Keep reading to learn how a stellar team presents this.)

Standards, strategies and goals are set by this director for the team and they then follow up on the set guidelines.

- **Standards:** All team members are fully engaged and have made routine the agreed-upon acquisition strategies.
- **Strategy:** The team implements the seven Supernova acquisition pieces: ninety Day Free Look, six Centers of Influence, four-member Mastermind Group, two Niches, two Community Boards, one Social Media Strategy, and VIPSA.
- **Goals:** Every team member has executed the seven acquisition strategies 100%.
- **Follow Up:** Director measures the success of the team's plan through the Gameboard. This ensures you are getting the results you want.

The **Director of Leadership** reports on the team's full production—assets gathered from whom, liability products in underwriting or approved, and what it means against the year-to-date production number. This Director also owns the 12-4-2 coaching model with the other team members, and reports any non-confidential information on professional achievements, etc. They set standards, strategies, and goals for the team and then track them.

- **Standard:** To create an environment where individuals can fail as well as succeed. To give honest feedback to each team member. To encourage everyone to help each other and leave their egos at the door.
- **Strategy:** Encourage growth of your business through the rule of reciprocity (i.e., if you give an extremely high level of service the client will want to help you in return by giving you introductions).
- **Goal:** To develop the skills, knowledge, and confidence of the team and help them achieve their goals.
- **Follow Up:** Daily stand-up meeting and weekly team meetings to measure the goals.

One Team's Take on the Scoreboard

One of the finest examples of the Scoreboard I've ever seen is Chris Brooke's team, Brooke, Smith & Associates. This high-performing practice has been growing spectacularly for years. They bring new clients in through a deliberate—even mechanized—process. They maintain acute visibility of new money opportunities within their current client community. They continuously assess, and re-assess, their production potential...not annually, quarterly, or even monthly. They reset their production trends in weekly, all-team meetings. And at the center of everything is a Gameboard. Or actually, three boards: their activities, their opportunities, and their operations. They have done what I want all teams to do: take each Supernova tool, implement it with intent and purpose, and then let it evolve to fit what you need it to do. Here's what Brooke, Smith & Associates did.

Activities

This is as close to classic Supernova as you're going to get. They created a clear and comprehensive view of activities, in their case, prospecting. In fact, they call it a Prospecting Board, and it has a column for every member of the team who touches acquisition. It records outbound calls, reaches, and appointments. For gathering introductions and tracking their movement, the board captures introduction inquiries across the spectrum, from current clients, social and board environments, and LinkedIn. The board captures the flow of introductions from first contact to new client relationship. It includes when an introduction is made, to and from whom, any ongoing contact during the dating process, and the final new client profile.

When I categorized their process as mechanized, it wasn't my description, it's theirs. In the words of Chris Brooke, "We call it 'manufacturing the client experience' and the process is rooted in the realities of an actual manufacturing operation. If you're making cars, and your goal is 100 a month, you better know how much steel you'll need, how many nuts and bolts you'll need, and how many person-hours it's going to take. Those are the inputs. If the inputs are off, the outputs fall. So we think in inputs." Chris goes on, "It takes X number of dials to get a reach and X number of reaches to get an appointment. It's a discipline that sounds simple to adhere to, but it's only simple if it's baked into the operation." Love it! But it's also more than a numbers' play. As his team reviews the numbers, they also have an ongoing conversation about the quality of the prospects and where they came from, which is another kind of input.

The intent here—and it is very intentional—is to move prospecting from an unconscious and random activity to a conscious and intentional activity. No one on his team will ever answer the question, "How many calls did you make today?" with "Oh probably about . . . " They will know precisely, and it's not the only thing they'll know.

Opportunities

They think of this board (and it's an Excel spreadsheet) as their inventory. It's the inventory of new prospects and new money from existing clients. In other words, it lists their growth opportunities, and it's reviewed by the full team every Monday. Everything is measured against the annual production goals, and it is updated every single Monday.

On the prospect side, they record the potential dollar amount based on the completed profile, and then the team assigns a probability number to the prospect. Sixty percent is probably the high end for new prospects, which reflects the reality of gathering assets.

Chris admits, "It's a subjective number, but it's not a wild guess either. We've been using it a long time and our instincts have been fine-tuned by iteration." For existing clients, opportunities are assigned a percentage as well, and some are easier to assess than others. Say a client has a significant rollover in the near future and says they intend to hand it to Chris' team. Pretty sure thing, right? Yes, but not 100%. Nothing gets 100%. Other opportunities are just inherently harder to quantify: an upcoming bonus, a liquidity event from a business sale, or even a sell order at a certain price. Those all get a lower percentage. That number, whatever it is, is the multiplier against the estimated dollar amount, which delivers an end number that becomes the projected production for that client or that prospect. They call it the "probability adjusted inventory" and in nearly two decades of practicing and refining it, they have dialed in that number. "We're rarely far off and frequently within a percentage point," says Chris.

Operations

The third board in the practice model measures operational performance, and that conversation happens every Friday. Every objective for every team member is added to that board. Maybe it's the hiring of a new CSA, or securing a lease on additional space, or entering a new market. Every operational objective is then segmented into steps, given a due date, and assigned to an individual. Every Friday, they talk about what they accomplished, the necessary next steps, who owns that, and, if there's a block, what can be done to remove it. It's collective accountability and reflects the ethos of the team. Nothing gets dropped on a CSA without first getting started as a task with a deadline. Chris' team uses Salesforce to keep track of everything.

Practices (or people) that don't grow either procrastinate or do more research. The enormity of an objective threatens them. High-performing practices and people translate their objectives into challenges, and then break them down into small steps. If all of this sounds too rigid for you, then you're reading it wrong. When asked who thrives in this system, Chris says, "People who respond to accountability and love change are more affected." Growth accelerates when there's a structure to support it. It's not about systems for the sake of systems; it's about a process that keeps operational drama out of the conversation so that growth can ignite. Just fabulous.

Management by Challenge

Collective challenges take performance discussions out of the closed office and into the larger team. Is there a role for a private performance management conversation? Only IF it's a real conversation in the true spirit of Supernova. One problem with the traditional model for performance management is that it offers nothing for the rest of the team. Nobody else has the opportunity to contribute and grow, and yet Supernova practices thrive when transparency trumps secrecy.

By making everything a challenge on the Giving Board, everyone knows what the other members of the team are focusing on. They can cheer for each other and offer support. Improvement opportunities are revealed in real time, with an explicit invitation for group-generated problem-solving. Maybe a role isn't right for someone, so talk about where they would fit better. Maybe the acquisition part of the business is bringing in too much and the exceptional service you promised is starting to look rather pedestrian. Nothing can be solved unless it is clearly identified.

CHALLENGE

In *The Supernova Advisor* we answered your call to "get me organized and keep me organized." It was a lot of work to build the folders, create the schedule, train the clients, and roll out the program. That same energy and focus must be invested in this part of the business model. This is the heart of *The Supernova Multiplier*. That same energy you put into developing your client service model must be matched to build the Five Star Model. If every team member just follows their role as described in this chapter, you will get the multiplier effect. It will take time, just like the service model did, but over time it will be a game changer. Your challenge is to:

- Assign all Five Star tasks
- Learn your values, responsibilities, and accountability tools
- Set your goals
- Set up the Giving Board and Scoreboard
- Set up your meeting schedule
- Execute on your plan.

4

90 Days 90 Prospects

One of the best ideas I've come up with wasn't even mine. In fact, it wasn't even an idea, because it wasn't, well, anything.

It was a miscommunication. What should have been an "error" message turned out to be a brilliant idea. An attendee at a coaching session misheard the explanation of 90 days, 90 prospects—more on this later.

As Supernova matured, we identified the general guideline that every FA should have somewhere in the neighborhood of 90 prospects in their pipeline, tops. So, what's a prospect? In this population of 90, the definition is pretty loose: it's someone with the assets that reach your current minimum, who knows you, knows something of how you work and will agree to learn more if asked. Ideally, a significant number of those individuals are those you connected with through one of your active marketing efforts—they were introduced by a Center of Influence, they were introduced through a Mastermind Group, or they are connected somehow to a board on which you serve. Obviously, of these 90 there are going to be prospects who are much closer to the new client finish line than others. Those potential clients earn more of your attention than the less well known or prospects in the infancy stage of your relationship.

Some FAs unrealistically estimate either a very high or very low number of prospects. Some say they have 300 prospects, which is as nuts as saying you have ten. When executed to precision with roughly 100 clients, Supernova 12-4-2 requires about two and a half days per week. That leaves **HALF** of the week for marketing and acquisition, and 90 prospects are plenty to carry in two and a half days.

Early on that was my conversation with a team in Louisville, KY. In coaching Supernova, the prospect pipeline is covered everywhere, and every FA seemed to be getting it with the exception of this one team. Turns out, it was a teaching moment and I was the student. The lesson was for the better of us all.

I'll hold on to his name because I don't want to embarrass him. But imagine my surprise while checking in on a coaching call, he said this: "Hey Rob, I've had this prospect I just knew was ready for Supernova service, but I couldn't get him to move out of some misplaced loyalty to his current advisor. So, I introduced him to your 90-day program, and I'll be danged if I didn't sign him up on day 91."

I said, "Um, excuse me, what 90-day program?"

"*Your* program to give highly qualified prospects a 90-day experience as a Supernova client. It totally works! Just brilliant."

"Well . . . thanks. Tell me exactly what you did again?"

That's how I heard all about my brilliant idea that wasn't mine at all but is, surprisingly, brilliant.

The Puppy Dog Close

In the world of sales, a "puppy dog close" is anytime you give a person an opportunity to use the product or hold the product before they buy it. Just like when you go into the pet store, the clerk says, "we have a lot of puppies here, but can you just hold onto this dog for a minute while I get this other one out?" By the time you leave the pet store that dog belongs to you.

When someone comes in for a new family car, a salesperson, using the same ploy, might say, "Why don't you take this little sports car home for the weekend?" If you go into a Mercedes dealer for a repair, you walk into a beautiful, top-of-the-line service center, you meet with your personal representative for maintenance, and they give you a beautiful brand-new loaner to take home in the hopes you will think about buying a new car. In our case, we can't give them a car, but we can give them with a WOW experience.

Here's a bonus multiplier! Inadvertently the FA I was coaching created an incredible tool for Supernova, the "90 Day Free Look" without even realizing it. Once a prospect has agreed to the 90-Day Free Look you know you have moved the needle much closer to a "yes" than a "no." When FAs get stuck this will always get them unstuck. If you've got someone on the hook, but you just can't close them, if the client is willing to have a 90-day trial, they may just become a client after they have enjoyed the ultimate client experience. With this kind of attention and service you have given them a tangible reason to move to you.

Simply stated, Supernova gives you the puppy that no else has. No one.

"No Means Know"

That's one of my Zig Ziglar favorites. In prospecting new clients the word "no" actually means "I need to know more before I make a decision." For many prospects you can help them know a whole lot more by showing them what Supernova service looks like. The 90-Day Free Look gives you that opportunity. To refresh your memory, here is the Supernova Service Model simply stated:

1. A folder system that includes:
   a. A pressboard classification folder for both the client and you including information about your team (bios, phone, email, address, and philosophy); see Figure 4.1 for template for folder system
   b. A broad-brush portfolio overview (second opinion)
   c. An abbreviated financial plan based on what you know about their assets and age, including their situation overview with a cash flow analysis for retirement planning
   d. An agenda for the first monthly call, and a detailed executive summary after each scheduled contact
   e. Blank pages for notes between calls.
2. Monthly contact for three months with two of the three scheduled contacts by phone, and ideally the third in person.

3. Rapid response to any questions they may have with a 1-hour response and 24-hour resolution during business hours.

It's a significant commitment—for both your prospect and you, and clearly not for everyone on your prospect list. The optimal candidate for the 90-Day Free Look is the fence-sitter who appreciates what you do but maintains some allegiance to their current advisor or is resistant to change or requires irrefutable proof to push through their resistance. Importantly, they also need to have enough trust in your team and you to reveal their assets and tell their story. What a great opportunity for you to show them the ultimate client experience. They see the contact ritual from the client side; they enjoy the attention given to their life situation, not just their asset level; they get 90 days

First Page	• Information about the prospect and their business • Contact information for introduction source
Second Page	• Planning you do for them or information about their portfolio
Third Page	• Agenda for the call/record of times you have met with them and notes
Last Page	• Blank lined paper for notes

Figure 4.1   Financial advisor's folders: prospects

First Page	• Critical Contact information • Enthusiastically Endorsed Providers
Second Page	• Performance Review or other benchmark/planning documents
Third Page	• Information about the 'Topic of the Month'
Fourth Page	• Introductions given or received • Cash Flow Analysis
Fifth Page	• Agenda for the next meeting
Last Page	• Blank lined paper for taking notes

Figure 4.2   Client folder: Give to prospects when they agree to a 90-Day Free Look

to experience a comparison between their current advisor and your team's commitment to premier client service.

And you?

You get to measure how invested and committed they are to playing their part in Supernova's success. If a client isn't going to make the appointments or engage in the conversations, remember they are a client who will diminish your brand. Better to find out before they are an actual client.

Checklist for Supernova Prospects

1. **Supernova Your Prospect List**—Determine who is a real prospect. You have to Supernova your prospect list—cross off those people who aren't interested, who don't need you, who don't see your value, and who haven't really been referred to you or don't fit into your niches.
2. **Build the Pipeline**—Create a spreadsheet of your prospects or put them on your Gameboard. Plan on making a call a day to either the prospect or the person introducing you to the prospect to set up a meeting.
3. **Improve Closure Rate by:**
   a. Improving the quality of the prospects. Focus on highly qualified prospects from introductions through valued COIs, your Mastermind Group, Community Boards, and Networks. Don't waste your time on people who don't want to hear from you. The maximum number should be 90—remember prospect follow-up is time consuming and your time is a limited resource.
   b. Improving the quality of people introducing you. The better the introduction, the higher the closure rate. A closure is directly proportional to the person who has referred you and how you're referred. A highly respected person (COI) who understands who is a good fit will dramatically improve your closure rate.

(continued)

(continued)

c. Shortening the amount of time to close. By focusing on service not product, you can minimize your time spent. One FA I used to work with would take six meetings to close. By making Supernova and service part of his presentation, he reduced his closure time to three meetings.

d. Offering the prospect a 90-Day Free Look.

Supernova by its nature is a process of determining what works versus what doesn't work, and we stay with what works. The 90-Day Free Look was the perfect example of adjusting the program to fit what works.

CHALLENGE

Challenge yourself with a 90-Day Free Look:

1. Pick three prospects who are on the fence and get them to try the 90-Day Free Look. Experiment and then send us your results to rdknapp@supernovaconsulting.com.
2. Supernova your prospect list. Segment out unqualified prospects and upgrade your introduction sources.

Using Centers of Influence to Grow Your Practice

It takes time for givers to build goodwill and trust, but eventually, they establish reputations and relationships that enhance their success.

Adam Grant

An authentic Supernova practice is never stagnant and is always growing. However, it needs to be controlled, intentional growth. One way to achieve that is through thoughtful introductions by professionals who know your practice, know you, and introduce you to qualified prospects. As I said in *The Supernova Advisor,* referrals (introductions) are generated through a process that is practiced, managed, coached, and measured. It is a value indicator of and value-add to your client relationship. It reflects the satisfaction and importance your clients place on your practice.

Clearly, a referral (introduction) can be valuable when it produces a new client for you. But it can also enrich the relationship between the referral and the person making the introduction. You can be a trusted professional in your client's life, ideally one with whom they share their inner circle. Referrals happen and they add value to the relationship in both directions. The path to a referral is more than a script. An effective referral (introduction) process is an extension of your respectful relationship with your client. It is characterized by two foundations: humility and candor.

It almost goes without saying that Centers of Influence who send you a steady flow of high-quality referrals are invaluable. These COIs can be other professionals, networkers, or just folks who want to help you succeed. They can introduce you to the "right type" of client—those who would appreciate premium service, accept the Supernova model of client/FA contact and meet your minimum asset standard. And yet most advisors report COI relationships that are inconsistent at best.

Do any of these situations sound familiar?

- They never have time to meet with you.
- They seem to have a lack of confidence in you and a hesitation to send business to you.
- You seem to send them more business than they send you.
- You only get sporadic referrals.
- The referrals they do send are not always a good fit.

Where do you begin? How do you identify possible COIs? Through our research and personal experience, we believe that the best COIs are individuals whom you have known for a while, you and they have a mutual respect for each other, and you share a thread of commonality. They are people who know you and trust you. Perhaps you went to the same college or played on the same team or were in the same clubs together in high school or college. They may be someone in your neighborhood either now or in your childhood. If you are active in a political party, place of worship, or volunteer opportunity, you can identify someone of interest there. If you don't have that advantage, you can look for introductions from your clients. They can introduce you to a highly recommended CPA (Certified Public Accountant), attorney, physician, or other professional. Don't get me wrong, this is not a suggestion to turn your friends into clients. That is for them to do. This is for you to turn the people in your circle into referral pipelines.

Michael Beers, a 17-year-veteran Financial Advisor and Supernova graduate, has an active referral network system in place:

> I'm very anti chasing a ton of COIs. I want exceptionally strong CPA. I want a very influential estate attorney. I want one exceptionally strong realtor. I don't need a long list. Only ones we think are important.

When meeting a person for the first time and explaining to them about introductions, they are going to automatically "size you up" and judge whether you are someone they can risk exposing to their clients. Would you give an introduction to a CPA who has a reputation for overcharging or stealing from their clients? Of course not! By the same token, a CPA doesn't want their clients—and their clients' life savings in the hands of an advisor until they are comfortable the person is honest, highly qualified, and offers great service.

Mike continues:

> When I would call an estate attorney, I typically have my CSA do it; she would say, "We'd like to schedule some time for our senior advisor to come meet with you. We are currently looking for an estate attorney to work with our clients. We work with high-net-worth clients and business owners who have very large liquidity events. We're looking for someone we can recommend to our clients. We'd like to send our advisors out to speak with you about how your firm can help us with that."
>
> We set up the interview so they need to sell themselves to us. They need to tell us why we would want to put our clients in front of them instead of making it feel like we're coming out to sell them on us. That has worked so much better than the other way around. We want them to feel like they need to be knocking on our door.
>
> We have a lot of clients, and we have a great brand in this city. The intrinsic message is, "We'd like to work with you, but we don't need to work with you. It's a privilege for us to work together. It isn't you or us; it's both of us." This has worked well.
>
> We made this approach with our current CPA. Right before tax season I took my wife to meet her (the CPA) and to see her reaction to the CPA. My wife had no idea. I told her I just wanted her to give me her honest impression and opinion. My wife absolutely loved her and now our clients love her. She later confided she felt like we were coming out to "kick the tires" on her practice.
>
> It really is just like you are coming to kick the tires on their business. This approach to a managed

exchange executed with professional deference promotes collegiality with neither of us heading for an immediate position of control. Potential professional contacts should feel like they're lucky to have us and vice versa.

We usually go to see prospective COIs first, and we say we would like to see your space and how you interact with your clients. This needs to be a mutual arrangement where everyone feels like they can trust the other person with their clients. I was talking with another advisor saying it's crazy that we advisors are always the ones putting our hand out. Make them put their hands out. Make them feel like they want to work with us. They're lucky to have us so they can say, I work with the Beers Consulting Group.

You should have a maximum of six Centers of Influence per financial advisor on your team. You should put aside two to three hours a month to have a quick in-person meeting with each of them. If you don't meet monthly, they tend to lose interest and stop giving you introductions.

Who Are Good Centers of Influence?

Natural COIs are the people who like you and trust you and send you introductions without you asking. They can be friends and family and the people that you knew before you got in the business. They are often clients in your practice who are already giving you introductions, e.g., if you came from Lilly, it could be the scientists at Lilly, or if you had a background in the restaurant service business, it's distributors, bar owners, etcetera.

Professional COIs are people with whom you can offer mutual introductions. CPAs, lawyers of various kinds (tax, estate planning, family), commercial and residential realtors, business brokers, business insurance agents (P&C, group health), etc. You want to have the best of the best, and they all should have high-net-worth clients and fit our minimums. Plan on having three COIs for all of these areas (CPAs, lawyers, insurance, etc.) to be effective. The number one person on this list is your lead CPA (they're up at bat). Your second CPA would be on deck, and your third CPA would be in the dugout. For the number one, you meet them for coffee every month—be prepared with some introductions; the second person, you'll meet four times a year, and the third, twice a year.

In his book, *Influence, The Psychology of Persuasion*, Robert Cialdini, Ph.D. has identified six key influencers of behavior.

Consciously or not, this is what a potential COI is looking for in you:

1. **Consistency**—Do you have a process in place the client can rely on for planning and meetings?
2. **Consensus**—Do you work with your clients to develop a cash flow analysis that you both agree on and keep (arrange) timely updates to keep them on course? Do you verbalize that process to your COIs?
3. **Authority**—Is your reputation stellar in the community? Do you have an active social media presence and publish work that is well written and well regarded?
4. **Similarity**—If you have chosen the right COI you will have commonality with them, and they can relate to you on the same level.
5. **Reciprocity**—Are you willing to give an equal number of quality introductions as they are?
6. **Scarcity**—Is yours a concierge practice that limits the number of clients? Do your clients see and value your practice as a very exclusive club?

The COI referral method works, but you must be consistent and patient. An FA that recently learned the process from me reported he had received both a $6 million and a $12 million referral from the same person in the same meeting using my methods. He couldn't believe the difference! It wasn't a new COI. The advisor had known this contact for years, but previously only a few small referrals had trickled in through the years.

But This Time It Was Different

What advice did I give him? I had him take the time to help the COI understand exactly how the FA treats the referrals he receives. Elementary, yes. Now, with the uncertainty of how the referral would be handled gone, the COI had the confidence to open his list of contacts. The advisor also made clear the financial requirements he had for the clients he accepted, so the COI could easily qualify which clients to refer. This is an important piece of the referral process. You don't want to have someone introduce someone to your practice and not be able to qualify them for the practice over something as clear-cut as not meeting your minimum of investible assets. The FA wasn't in the market for just any old referral. Quality over quantity. He offered exclusivity that was partially measured by net worth.

Back to Beers:

> I have one COI that has been our #1 referral source by far. This year alone we closed two 401(k)s, and a cash balance plan. We're in the process of another 401(k), a DV plan with cumulatively north of $50M in private client assets. She's also come on as a client. We made great efforts to sit down with her and show her how we do things and how we interact with our clients. Our close rate with her introductions is ridiculously high.
>
> Most of the referrals she's sending over to us have the potential to be worth north of $5M. A few were well north of $10M. I would say one is $20M plus we get the 401(k) plan. We tell our COIs we have some strict minimums, but we focus more on the number of individuals we bring in during the year. Also, the type of client we're looking to bring on has to fit our mold.
>
> We interview a potential client just as they are interviewing us. We can't spend this much time, attention and focus and working with a family (we always take families) if we just brought on everybody who wanted to work with us. We make it a little sexier saying we don't market, we don't advertise, you're not going to get mailers from us, you're not going to see any ads in the newspapers for us. We're 100% introduction-driven. I think that appeals to that client type. That's precisely what they want—highly

personalized service done very efficiently, highly reputable and very systematic. Everybody knows where we are in the relationship. I think the COIs like that.

This particular COI is also looking for a succession plan in her practice. She understands our team is very supportive of her. We've given her many referrals for estate planning. That relationship is very reciprocal. We've both benefited tremendously. We like each other. We have a good rapport with each other. The structure is there. The sense of focusing on a client is there. The Supernova model helps you narrow down and concentrate on a few good COIs rather than having a 1,000 of them that never offer you a meaningful or fruitful relationship with them. Find a few good COIs and take care of them.

We purposefully make it a point to sit down with our clients and explain we hired an outside consultant to review our practice and this evaluation propelled us to improve service to our clients. It emphasizes how we are invested in our clients' experiences. Our goal is to make every client feel like they're our only client. Their perception of our service is everything to us.

We've dropped that tagline with a lot of our COIs. It resonated with this one in particular because she used to work with a very large law firm. She left that practice and formed her own business with her husband. She's recruited some much younger attorneys and we've just really hit it off. I think the more we have shown her that we are a formidable team with a lot of depth on the bench the closer we have become.

Kind of that Jerry McGuire philosophy of "less is more." It works really, really well. I think one of the biggest advantages of Supernova is the skill ability of your practice. Being able to structure and control the frequency in which you're contacting people, how you're touching them, the subject matter you cover with them. If you do it right, it opens up time to allow you to make a client feel like they're your only client. We have been introduced to qualified prospects by our COIs, and the premium service model and personal touch are incredibly attractive to them.

Clients also appreciate the structure around every element of our interaction whether it was the phone calls, the structure of our client reviews, the contents of their folder; or something else. I think without having gone through, here's your folder, here's how we're going to review, here's your calendar, here's the structure, we would not have gotten certain relationships. If we would have done what every big team did and said, "We're on the Baron's List, we've got a lot of people, we've got CFPs, CFAs, CEMAs," we'd still look like every other big team in Columbus. We are differentiated by that structure around how we're going to interact with you at a personal level. Our feedback includes comments like, "Yeah, I've never seen that before, I've never heard that before, I like that idea of frequent contact." It was a big win for us.

Ask Yourself These Questions:

Do your COIs know how you will treat their clients?

The most significant reason COIs don't give referrals is a lack of history or knowledge about you. They may know you, but they don't truly understand how you operate. Invite them to come into your office, introduce them to your team, let them sit on the other side of your desk and show them how you treat the referrals you receive. The little things, even the way they will be introduced, matter.

Do your COIs know the specific type of client you are seeking?

Don't leave your COIs guessing as to the type of client you would like to have and therefore the person to whom you would like an introduction. Be as specific as possible. Otherwise, you're leaving it up to their imagination. They may think they've been sending you great referrals when in reality you've been getting prospects that don't meet your minimum.

Do you meet with your COIs regularly?

You have a regular schedule for meetings with your clients. The same should be true for your COIs. After you have identified a person that you would like to have as a COI, approach them to see if they would be available and interested in a regularly scheduled monthly meeting. Most professionals are interested in growing their practice and are more than willing to meet with someone who is another qualified professional. When your COI meetings become a habit, you will have a more predictable flow of referrals.

Five Steps to Approaching a COI

First Step: If you know the person already, you can just call them and set up a time to meet. In the case of someone you don't know, have a third party give you an introduction either through an in-person or phone meeting or an email or social media introduction. You want to get a folder to them that contains all your pertinent information. Explain what you are looking for and ask them if they would be interested. Go ahead and interview them and let them question you. Share your story and specifics of your practice, mission statement, and goals including the minimum number of assets you accept and the maximum number of clients you have. Include frequency and length of meetings, what they should expect from you, and the number of prospects you would like to keep in rotation. To keep the COI relationship current, plan on meeting them once a month.

Second Step: Plan the meeting in their office—ideally meeting their team and giving everyone a copy of *The Supernova Advisor* so they can learn how you run your practice. Explain that in particular, you would like to meet with everyone who would engage with your client.

Third Step: Introduce them to your team. Invite them to your office for a presentation with the purpose of showing them what differentiates your practice from others, what premium service looks like, and how you deliver it to your clients. At this meeting introduce the Five Star Model.

Fourth Step: Teach them to use the "Enthusiastically Endorsed Model"[1] for every client. Ask them: "Can you enthusiastically endorse your CPA?" and your COI will do the same by asking their client, "Can you enthusiastically endorse your FA?"

Fifth Step: Finally, have your first monthly meeting with an agenda and ideally an introduction for them. At this meeting schedule your next session to help you keep the process going. Make these monthly COI meetings ritualized on your monthly calendar just as you would any client appointment. Your CSA/CA should schedule these appointments. Not including your CSA/CA in the COI process is a major failure point. Get the scheduling out of your hands and into the hands of your administrator.

There are three ways you can give each other introductions: in person, by phone, or through an email or social media introduction. If a client was in need of a referral, I always insisted on giving my clients three names before they made a choice on which one they wanted to use. It's just a best practice that will elevate you above other advisors. You don't want your clients to feel like you are pushing anyone on them. This process may seem time-consuming, but is well worth the time invested. Most successful COI relationships take years to develop properly. This process takes a couple of months and can get the same results. There are no shortcuts here.

An example of a team doing COIs the right way is Ken Shapiro and Tom Livaccari who started as partners in 2002 at Merrill Lynch, and after two years went to another firm. When I started coaching them in 2009 they had $150 million in assets. They have since grown that to $800 million using the Supernova approach. Revenues were 1.1 million and now they are annualizing at over $4 million. They had 100 clients then, and now they have 50. They were FAs then, and now they are Private Wealth Advisors. Minimums were $1 million, and now they're $10 million. And they credit a great deal of that progress to Supernova. They only work with entrepreneurs who are having a liquidity event.

Ken says:

> When we meet with a COI we request they meet with us once a month or sometimes once a quarter. We tell them about our experience with Supernova and how we run our practice and what we're teaching our clients. We treat most of these guys (that we know have a good connection with clients) like they are Supernova clients and have one-on-one quarterly or monthly breakfasts or late afternoon coffees that are on the calendar with a folder. Most are monthly; very few are quarterly. If they are interested in learning about our process and Supernova, we teach them how to do it and we give them the book as a gift.
>
> Last year we purchased 40 books and gave them to everyone. We believe if a COI is in an accounting practice, there's no reason they can't take on these concepts for their business. I would say, "You've told us you're impressed with what we're doing, here's the book." That is the foundation upon which we based our practice. I don't know how many COIs or prospects have read it, but we thought it would be an impactful way to reinforce what we're doing and also help them at the same time. I would say most of the people stick to it. When they have to cancel a meeting with us they always apologize for having to cancel. Before we started doing Supernova we would spend time chasing the CPA around to get an appointment and say, hey, Michael, I haven't seen you around in a very long time. Let's get a cup of coffee, back and forth, back and forth, and you never meet. With this approach, we have 80% of the meetings and the 20–30% who don't say they're swamped and feel guilty. It changes the dynamics.

This is one of my favorite stories from working with Ken and Tom. Ken told me:

We had met with a CPA inconsistently over several years. We met with him and explained what we were doing, i.e. 12-4-2; formal planning and rapid response and that we would like a more meaningful relationship with him. We requested he meet with us monthly. After the second meeting he referred a client who was selling his business. They were one of five people pitching this referral prospect for business. Their prospect was selling his business for $60 million and needed to hire someone to help him. Ken and Tom were second or third in the presentation line. And at the end of their presentation, they handed the prospect the folder, and said, "This is your client folder with a section here for notes, and another for agendas for our meetings." Then they went through the 12-4-2 process (we'll be in touch with you every month, do a financial plan, and every month we'll talk about this plan and have a system for following up and making sure it all gets done). The client said, "What?" in disbelief. And they went back through it again. He was shocked. He said no one else had talked about service. They had all talked about performance, but none had talked about service. The prospect said, "Cancel the other appointments, I'm going to go with you guys!" It wasn't about a presentation; it was service that won it. He's now an $80 million account! When the COI found out they had won the account, and why the prospect was so impressed in the interview he continued to refer people to them.

I want to end this chapter by saying only you know what works for you. Sometimes FAs lack the confidence to follow through on their convictions. Don't let that happen to you! Follow my template as laid out here and you will be successful.

CHALLENGE

Contact an existing COI and set up the Monthly Model. Pitch the Supernova model to them and ask for an introduction. Train a COI how to introduce your team.

NOTE

1. The Enthusiastically Endorsed Model (see example at the end of this book) is a list of professional providers that you create based on enthusiastically endorsed recommendations by more than one client. The FA should keep a master list of these professionals. This list can be beneficial to new people moving into town who need everything from a realtor to a dentist. Whenever your client would like to replace one of these providers, you provide them with three names and introductions to people you know who would be suitable for their situation. These endorsed providers are prime candidates to become COIs for you.

CHAPTER

6

Niches

After you adopt the Supernova Model and have more free time, where else will you find great, high-quality introductions? Niche marketing will take your Supernova process to the next level. This is your next Supernova Multiplier.

Why are niches so important? They provide you with an opportunity to be introduced to qualified prospects with a high degree of established credibility, both theirs and yours. In his book *Influence*, Robert Cialdini notes one of the critical elements to connecting with people is having similarity. When you become a specialist in any area you are automatically trusted because you speak their particular business or industry language, you have a working knowledge of their company or field, and, most of all, are in their circle because you are already working with their colleagues.

In Indianapolis, we had a number of advisors specializing in local corporations where the niche members met their minimum requirements for their practice. They developed a COI inside that niche and grew their practices dramatically through introductions using this model.

At Eli Lily, Simon Property Group, UPS, and Dow Elanco we had great success because our FAs were "specialists" within these companies' employee circles. Other niches not tied to major corporations that worked for us were authors, cardiologists, car dealers, lawyers, university and hospital staffs.

In asking the average financial advisor what their niche or niches are, the usual answer is "I don't have one" or they have a very vague or general answer such as: "retirees," "business owners," "wealthy people." From that point, we have to drill down in order to find a real affiliation.

Here's the problem with those generalized groups. They find little or no affiliation with you. When you specialize in a niche such as scientists at Eli Lilly, they understand you are a specialist in their retirement plan and benefits program. They have been referred to you by a trusted colleague and immediately see value in a relationship with you.

What is a Niche?

- A niche is a target or circle of opportunity—a congregation or nest of like-minded people, engaged in an activity for their mutual benefit. The Business Directory defines it as, "concentrating all marketing efforts on a small but specific and well-defined segment of the population. As a strategy, niche marketing is aimed at being a big fish in a small pond instead of being a small fish in a big pond." Visually, they are circles and being on the inside is your goal.
- To target a niche or circle, you need to identify the commonality, group, industry, or company and become immersed in their world so that you are considered one of them. You talk their language, enjoy their company, become part of their tribe, and fit in the group.

Craig Dobbs is a good example that comes to mind. He was a very successful financial advisor and #1 on Barron's Institutional List. He had a relationship with the Sheet Metal Workers International Association because both of his parents were union members. Craig grew up in the union and admired its leaders and members. He grew up speaking their language. That was unusual for a member of the financial services community but he made it work. His business exploded when he focused on unions. He was accepted by them as one of their own and he persisted in pursuit of their best interests. He gradually became the authority on their retirement plans and established a larger and growing business in that market.

Two Types of Niche: Natural/Organic and Target

The first type of niche group is natural or organic. You have niches that you develop within your practice. They are organic, they grow from within your practice—either due to your current clients or your personal interests or background. When I first started at Merrill Lynch, I was coming out of the Navy and still drilled on the weekends. Those that shared weekend duty with me became my natural niche. The officers that I drilled with became my friends and eventually we saw ourselves as a large family. Since I was one of them, they trusted me with their financial planning and I did business with many of them for years.

Natural niches are the former careers, industries, companies, or commonalities that you came from. Mine was the Navy. This was a natural niche for me, having served 3.5 years in active duty and seven as a reserve with a rank of Lt. Commander. I was automatically accepted. I spoke their language and they trusted me.

Inside each niche you need to develop at least one Center of Influence. Just to remind you, COIs are people you probably already have as clients. By definition they like you, trust you, and are willing to introduce you without asking. A niche can also be referred to as a nest. The nest, for example, might be a group of cardiologists in a partnership. If you were previously in the medical profession, this would be a great resource. For example, if you were hired from Baxter Labs, you'd go back Baxter for clients; you already speak their language and you know the company, their benefits, and the retirement structure. This is an example of a natural niche—already being on the inside of the circle is an extraordinarily convenient position—speaking the language, knowing the business. The bonus is most of your former colleagues would be highly qualified as prospects.

Target/External Niches

Target or external niches are those that you identify from the outside. You are looking into their circle and right now you are wanting to find an opening. Jumping in without first investing your time and efforts to learn their business, language, and culture will likely land you on the outside, permanently. As the saying goes, "You only have one chance to make a good first impression." Research. Learn. Prepare. Go for it.

When UPS first went public, their managers needed help investing. The stock they had been given over the years was suddenly worth millions. They had no idea what to do with it. I took the opportunity to hire a UPS manager from the finance department to work at Merrill Lynch. I helped him with seminars for those UPS executives on how to minimize risk and on estate planning; we were able to help a large number of UPS employees and built a nice practice for the former UPS manager and now new Merrill Lynch FA. This was a calculated, strategic move. Had we tried to crack the exterior of the UPS circle as an outsider, we would have failed.

This UPS program became a target niche. When I went to different cities in my region, I would identify a team within each office who knew how to develop business. They were then given a crash course on UPS and taught how to successfully target the UPS niche in their area. They were like little swat teams in cities like Louisville, St. Louis, and Little Rock. We rolled it out and it was very successful. The new UPS clients were delighted. We set up their trusts and family foundations, and handled the other fiscal planning needs that would allow them to pass their financial values on to their children. When you know that there is a financial event within one of your niches you can use it to create business for your team and you.

In Indianapolis, a large pharmaceutical company like Eli Lilly would be a good example of a target niche. Another example would be a major hospital like IU Med Center, since it includes the department heads and affiliated groups of specialists, e.g. a group of cardiologists or anesthesiologists, who enjoy hospital privileges. Everyone associated with the Med Center is a potential client and they can be further vetted for investible asset minimums based on specialty or position.

The perfect niche must have a sufficient number of potential clients in it who see you as a trustworthy and knowledgeable authority in financial planning and have the assets to meet your minimum. The benefit of a COI inside the circle is a regular stream of introductions.

When I started, I had ten niches, very few accounts, and nothing but time. I continued to work those ten my whole career. Unless they are connected and there is a significant overlap of drill-down information, it would be a very difficult to be an expert in ten circles. And this is what you want to be, the expert. You may not have all the answers, but you know where to find them, who to ask, how the company works. For more seasoned FAs, I would recommend starting with a minimum of two niches—one natural and one target. If those two are right for you and you invest the time and effort it takes to learn and understand the company or industry, that should be enough. You know enough to be comfortable and conversational around the financial benefits, retirement planning options, etc., that are germane to that niche. If you have the time to be knowledgeable and conversant in more, then you are ready to add to your circles of competence.

When seasoned Wealth Advisor Ben Altman signed up for some coaching I was invited to a meeting in Chicago with his real estate Mastermind Group. I sat next to an individual who worked for a fast-growing disrupter in the real estate business called CoStar Realty Group. CoStar evaluates commercial real estate in the United States and then offers that information as a service to real estate companies that buy their research, saving potential buyers from having to go out and assess the properties themselves. This individual acts as a COI for Ben within CoStar. He introduces Ben to qualified prospects who need a top-notch financial advisor. Companies like CoStar represent the kind of opportunities that we can target to build an internal network. It is a very important relationship.

Another FA that I worked with at Merrill took the work we were doing and turned it into a very successful practice. John Hurlow started working with me in the late 90s. He left Merrill to start his own firm in 2002 and applied the niche principle to his practice. John said:

I know most people do not promote trying to make a geographic area your niche...but I sent out to conquer Bloomington, Indiana and that is what we have done. We have a second office in Indianapolis, we have hired two more FAs this year, and we are killing it! Today we are a fee-only RIA with $250 Million AUM. I have served on countless non-profit boards over the years and we have a very well-defined process for servicing clients which we call our CFO process (Coordinated Financial Overview) which includes all the segmentation and client service principles that I learned from Rob.

Steps Needed to Get Into a Niche

1. Learn the company's benefit plan. You have to become an expert on the company or business including HR benefits, retirement options, and stock options. Read their annual report. Be an expert on the things that are important to the people within that company. Knowing the details will enhance your value.

2. Learn the language of the company. Every company has acronyms, and you have to learn them. FAs, CAs, CSAs, admin, service—whatever they call their people, scientists, VPs, etc. If you use the wrong term, you could look like an outsider at best and at worst offend them. When I was a young FA we would have wholesaler presentations and if they referred to us as registered reps instead of FAs they immediately lost the interest of everyone in the audience.

3. Understand the culture of the company. Here are some examples of cultures you need to understand before you can understand the company:

   a. Merck had a famous culture which is symbolized by a statue in the front of their headquarters of a young boy leading a middle-aged blind man. The company accidentally discovered the cure for river blindness, which only affects people in remote parts of Africa.

Dr. Roy Bagelos, President of Merck, decided to make the drug Mectizan available without charge because those who needed it most could not afford to purchase it. Annually the Mectizan Donation Program reaches more than 250 million people and more than 2 billion treatments have been donated since 1987. The statue is there as a reminder of their commitment to helping others in need. Their mission—"To discover, develop and provide innovative products and services that save and improve lives around the world." When asked why he would commit to a drug that would never make a profit he said, "I had no choice. My whole life has been dedicated to helping people and this was it for me." Jimmy Carter stated, "Merck's gift to the World Health Organization is more than a medical breakthrough—it is truly a triumph of the human spirit."[1]

b. McKinsey & Company, which has a culture of excellence, fires the bottom 10% of their staff every year with the express purpose of making everyone understand that mediocrity will not be accepted.

4. Develop a dependable COI inside the niche and meet with them monthly. They should be respected within the niche and proud to be doing business with you. Their association with you should carry some weight in both directions.

5. Be highly visible in the community in that niche even to the point of having an office inside that company where you can work and meet with people because you're such a help. You want them to think of you as the backup HR department.

6. Have a strong relationship with the HR department. Learn their benefits package better than they know it. Most high-level employees don't know the benefits that are available to them nor the retirement packages or process. You can be their resource person. You can be helpful for things like consulting on retirement transitions, promotions, and layoffs. When I served as a Merrill Lynch Managing Director my FAs were given office space at both Lilly and Chrysler because they trusted us to really help their people. We became an extension of the HR Department.

You met Ken Shapiro and Tom Livaccari in the last chapter. They have embraced and instituted this concept to its fullest in their practice. Ken states,

> We specialize in technology groups. Last year we brought in $120 million and were able to leverage our Centers of Influence by setting up meetings each month that worked with our technology prospects. This validated what we knew, who we knew and how we could help them.

Internal Niches

Niches can be areas of internal specialization, a circle within a circle. In the case of your own firm, you have the opportunity to be the internal specialist all high-level employees go to for any advice that HR can't answer. I know managers/advisors who don't have a clue as to what to do when they are ready to retire. They are basically on their own. And surviving spouses—where do they turn? You can be there to help them with advice and guidance

How to Develop a New Niche Script

- Identify a client who could be a Center of Influence inside a potential niche. Let them (in this example, a car dealer) know that you need their advice and would like a few minutes of their time. Tell them you are considering adding more car dealers to your practice. Explain that they are an ideal client because:
  - They are easy to deal with
  - They understand risk
  - They are used to making decisions
  - They take your advice
  - They meet your minimum.
- You then say, "Do you think it makes sense at this time to add more car dealers to my practice?" More than likely, they will say yes.
- That is when you ask the key question: "If you were me, how would you go about adding more car dealers to my practice?"

- Then you keep quiet and listen. Let the client, in this case, tell you how to get in front of other car dealers.
- If the car dealer has no ideas how to do that you can say, "When do you normally meet?" "Is there an association of car dealers?" "What charities do you guys support I could support?" "How do you suggest I go about connecting with them?"

If you really run into a roadblock merely ask them to think about it and follow up next time. "Don't forget, I am never too busy to help people like you." At worst, you have planted the seed that you would like to have more car dealers in your practice.

One other thought on your niche. Almost every market segment has a publication specific to it and many of the publications are free. To make the point, there is a publication called *Pit and Quarry* for quarry owners and those in the aggregates industry. There are multiple publications for physicians. Go to www.modernmedicine.com to sign up for the free digital magazine. How about looking at www.freetrademagazines.com to see a list of targeted publications? If you have a niche, you will be more effective in the circle if you can speak the lingo. Reading publications specific to your niche will allow you to learn the "language."

He Found a Niche Based on His Passion

Having a career as a financial advisor, manager, regional director and now coach has given me the opportunity to get to know a lot of amazing financial advisors and their teams. One that stands out is Patrick Renn from Atlanta. I actually met him quite by accident through the Supernova members-only Advanced Learning Library we created in 2005. Patrick has the distinction of being the only advisor that we know of to implement Supernova just by reading the book, using the Supernova Scheduling Tool and following our "lessons" on the site.

One day, Cindy Beuoy, who runs the site, said to me, "Rob you have to get in touch with Patrick. He has been a member since day one and he is doing everything you say but hasn't had a single coaching session with you. Let's find out how he did it. It would make a great testimonial for Supernova."

So we scheduled a call and Patrick told me his story. He was first introduced to Supernova at a Raymond James meeting (he is an independent agent for RJ). Everyone at the meeting was gifted my book *The Supernova Advisor* and told it was a must-read. Patrick read the book and decided he liked the ideas and processes it presented and immediately plunged into setting his minimum thresholds, maximum number of clients and screens for clients. Patrick is a great example of someone integrating Supernova. We loved interviewing Patrick for an article about how to get started with Supernova, but left it there.

Time passed and like a lot of Supernova advisors he took the process a step further.

I was always interested in charitable planning for my clients. Over the years I have served on many nonprofit boards and thought it was very fulfilling to help these charities build their endowment to meet their day to day expenses. I always ask them to look at the bigger picture and imagine what it would look like if they had an endowment large enough to live off the yearly increase. That's the amount of money they need to raise. It makes sense to not have to scramble around every year just to raise enough cash to keep operating.

About 8–10 years ago I was looking at my clients, reflecting on what the next decade would look like, and realized the one thing they all had in common was a desire to create a charitable trust. I realized I was getting referrals to like folks who had an ability and desire to give back to their communities in a big way. I think it's important to use the term Estate Planning or Generational Planning and not "tax planning." We are trying to keep a family's assets intact to allow it to grow for generations. Many of my clients are concerned their beneficiaries will not have the same vision as they have and will either spend the assets or lose them through divorce. What we do ensures the family's money stays in the family and every generation benefits from it.

I really love this work because I find it challenging and continually changing as the tax law changes. By accidentally focusing on this area I had become known in Atlanta as the go-to person for that kind of work. I have even written a book, *Finding Your Money's Greater Purpose (How to Make Your Legacy Count)*, with all proceeds donated to charity.

On the boards I have served on, I usually work with the development director and planned-giving director. Whenever there is a case that is technically over their heads they refer the donor to me, which can result in a new client. One year I was involved in Special Olympics and I was asked to help them with their investment strategy around their endowment. We secured some sponsors but were still looking for more. One of them introduced me to a guy who was very interested in helping us. He owned multiple retail locations of a well-known brand and was very generous to the cause. We invited his entire family to participate in that year's event and they continued to do so for many events.

Years later, when he decided to sell his company he called me to see if I could help him with the sale. He had financial advisors he had worked with but felt he needed someone who specialized in asset transfer/estate planning. I prepared to make a pitch to manage his assets and he just looked at me and said, "I'm not one to get involved in all the nitty gritty details, you have the reputation of being able to handle this kind of thing so just give me the forms and I will turn it all over to you."

Having this kind of a reputation is worth more than a big office, fancy stationery, or having multiple accreditations. Don't get me wrong; all of those things are nice but your reputation in the community, in a niche, will help you grow a successful business.

I wasn't looking for anything more than to help a cause I was interested in. It turned out I was very good at what I did and my reputation speaks for itself. I think when you show people who you are they will be naturally attracted to that and want to do business with you.

I think Patrick is dead on.

CHALLENGE

Create three niches:

1. One natural (from your background—college, team, club, interest, previous profession, or employer) or organic from inside your practice by expanding on a cluster of current clients (they already know you and your level of service, they can make introductions for you, you are already versed in their specific financial picture).
2. One target or external niche (what interests you, or an identified underserved market, or a company or industry with a shift in employee status or benefits like UPS, for example).
3. An internal niche or specialization (e.g. in 401Ks, mortgages, retirement, stock option plans, stock purchase plans). This will increase your effectiveness, desirability, pool of potential clients, and indispensability in your niche.

   If you are newer in the business and really looking to grow, I would consider creating four to six niches.

NOTE

1. Sources: http://www.merck.com/about/featured-stories/mectizan .html; Michael Useem. 1999. *The Leadership Moment: Nine True Stories of Triumph and Disaster and Their Lessons for Us All.* Crown Business; http://www.nytimes.com/1987/10/22/world/merck-offers-free-distribution-of-new-river-blindness-drug.html; and http://www .worldbank.org/en/news/feature/2014/07/03/forty-years-later-the-extraordinary-river-blindness-partnership-sets-its-sights-on-new-goals

CHAPTER 7

Mastermind Groups

f you are committed to working the Supernova Process the importance of your building deeper, more meaningful relationships with your COIs will become very evident, very quickly. As you fully implement monthly in-person COI meetings these relationships will grow stronger, more meaningful, and more productive. To take this to the next level use your COI introduction pipeline to create a Mastermind Group. This is an opportunity to help you help others in an even deeper, more profound way with the natural byproduct being a stronger and improved practice. Remember it's never about getting referrals, it's always about helping others. There is a distinct difference between a referral and an introduction. A referral is sending one person to another. Impersonal. Uninvolved. Less potential for you to personally create value for others. Building a reputation as a critical connector will create the right brand and is the key to becoming a true multiplier.

What Is a Mastermind Group?

Mastermind Groups have been around for centuries.[1] A Mastermind Group helps your peers and you achieve success. Each member of the group agrees to build a business plan, set challenging goals within that plan, and strive to achieve those goals. By sharing your plan and goals you create group accountability and a support team that helps you reach those goals. The group requires commitment, confidentiality, a non-compete agreement, honesty, and a willingness to both give and receive advice. Napoleon Hill offered the following definition of a Mastermind Group in his two books *The Law of Success* and *Think and Grow Rich*: "A Mastermind Group is the coordination of knowledge of two or more people, who work toward a definite purpose, in the spirit of harmony. No two minds ever come together without thereby creating a third, invisible intangible force, which may be likened to a third mind" (the Master Mind).

Members of a Mastermind Group should be enthusiastically endorsed professionals in your community who you can refer to and who can refer to you. By definition you meet regularly (monthly) with the sole purpose of helping each other grow your individual practices. Think of it as a group of friends who meet to make each other smarter.

Typically, there are four to ten people in a Mastermind Group. You may have six, but you don't necessarily need to have that many. The quality of your members is more important than the quantity.

One of the original Mastermind Groups started with Thomas Edison, Thomas Burroughs, Henry Ford, and Harvey Firestone in Ft Myers. It was purely an intellectual exchange. Clearly, they all wanted to make money and were incredibly rich people in their time, but they were also fascinated by each other's minds, and their ability to create the future.

Your Mastermind Groups should operate the same way. Invite those who will inspire intellectual curiosity exchanges, be eager learners, be enthusiastic about being in the group, be able to understand and able to reciprocate with their time and ideas. They should be "givers," not takers, as described by Adam Grant in his book *Give and Take*; each member should help each person create business; ideally this will be business outside of your particular area of specialty but complementary to your business.

There are a few important elements for choosing good people for your Mastermind Group:

- You like them. You trust them. They have or would make introductions for you without you asking.
- They're in a similar situation and similar stage of life: age, work ethic, family. The kind of person that you'd like to have over for a Sunday barbecue.
- Ideally, they should be professional service providers at the same level in their respective industries. You have something useful to offer each other. My client can be your client *quid pro quo*. If I have a $10 million client, I feel comfortable introducing them to my CPA, estate planning attorney, business broker, realtor, etc.

One of the best examples of successful and valuable Mastermind Groups is from one of my favorite FA clients, Alissa Quinn. She said to me:

> One of the things I did early in my career, prompted by being the only female FA in my office (out of 25 financial consultants) was to surround myself with other high executive women and female business owners in a group called The Professional Women's Network. This was an exclusive professional women's group dedicated to helping each other develop our businesses in a collaborative process.

When asked how and why a Mastermind Group had been instrumental in her success she replied:

> A number of years into it we found just having a referral or "leads" group was limiting in the sense that people who are professional and maybe women in particular feel most comfortable making a referral to someone they trust. It really is about a professional group developing and building trust. As a result, referrals and introductions are much more comfortable. Fast forward about 5 years into that group, one of the members broke down into more of a raw conversation and our tagline was "we went from soup to souls." It was then that real issues, real friendships,

and real personal connections were happening. Then as a result, business was being done.

A number of years later, I started another high-level female executive network. At the time, you were either pegged on the mommy track or the career track. I felt very strongly about doing both, so I put together a smaller group of women who truly believed in being able to have a well-balanced family life with an executive or entrepreneurial career. Again, the focus was on the deeper friendships, and as a result, we were much more comfortable building business, attending black tie affairs, and introducing each other to potential prospects and COIs. Those are ways we connect very candidly with follow-up.

What really drove the point home about the Mastermind Group's value were her comments about trust.
She said:

> For me the Mastermind Groups were only a beginning point, but the beginning point was developing the trust. Once the trust was established, it was making the introductions and connections with those COIs.

By utilizing the Supernova process she really got to know potential and existing clients, genuinely helping them, which in turn revealed additional assets.
She said:

> Then we do our SN process, we get together with those folks for a quick introductory meeting, we share our business platform and model. We're always seeking to understand first what that individual's needs are from a business point-of-view. If they're an entrepreneur, what needs do they have that aren't being met, what are their challenges, problems? We're always trying to be problem solvers for their particular challenges. Once we go through how we can help them, then we're utilizing our model and

showcasing our capabilities. We have a brochure; we walk them through the steps of what we do, how we do it, our financial planning collaborative process. Then, if there is a reason to connect, we'll follow up with a strategic first appointment for a financial goal analysis. We're off and running!

"For us," she said, "Mastermind Groups are simply used to develop very strong personal professional relationships that allow us to make introductions and connections to other COIs in the business community. We use that list of folks to connect with all our prospects."

Mastermind Groups are also a great way to create niches, as discussed in Chapter 6.

Alissa told me she recently started a third group to focus on a specific niche that has a very different mix— women who have all gone through some health issues. It's a very strategic group. And again, she uses this group to develop deep relationships and then utilizes those for her Supernova Process.

Bonus Multiplier!

Alissa again:

We are very strong users of social media. We use LinkedIn. Once we meet a professional COI, we'll connect with them on LinkedIn. Then we use LinkedIn strategies to reach out to them on a personal basis, "Would you be open to a cup of coffee? We'd love to learn how we might be able to help you in your business development, and at the same time be happy to share what we do and for whom we do it."

We use these Mastermind Groups simply to get a foot in the door. It is a much warmer introduction. Then we use our very structured process for a meeting with them in our office. We use the blue folders; we have the list of all the strategic things we're uncovering about their particular situation. We are then going through the FGA process, gathering all the assets and closing the business.

For 25 years my initial group met for an early breakfast in the boardroom at a local upscale hotel. Everyone would answer 3 very simple questions: What's new, what do I have to give, what do I need?

We had another program called a "Barn Raising," where each person would give a personal and professional update then answer the question: What do I have to give, what do I need? One example, I was the FA of the group, and had been asked to become the sales manager in our office. I was completely shocked by that. It was an offer on the table very early in my professional career, and at the time, I thought there would be no way I'd even remotely consider doing it. Not only was I the only female FA in the office, I was very young and the other FAs quite my senior. The manager asked me and it was a manager I didn't think would want my input. We met at a local business and everyone who could come, came. We went around the table and strategized. What's the upside/downside, what are all the options? We had a very collaborative discussion. I remember one woman who is an attorney said, "I've known you for 10 years, what's the worst that could happen? If you don't do this, I think you're going to think in your entire career, why didn't you do this? Do it, you're a busy person." I had a 4-year-old son at the time, and I was expecting my second child (I hadn't told anyone in my professional circle yet). Give a busy person something to do and they'll find a way to get it done. Take the job, if you don't like it a year from now, stop doing it.

That completely turned around the way I was thinking about it because I put 10 women executives in a room and we had a strategic conversation about it. I took the job for a year, I'm glad that I did it. I realized early on that wasn't the avenue I wanted to pursue, but it was an outstanding decision that I chose to do it.

We do our morning breakfast meetings, more board-room style, but if we have an issue that is raised, then we do the Barn Raisings. The Barn Raisings can be at someone's home, at a business club, off-site or on-site. They develop and deepen trust/relationships. You're baring your soul to challenging issues.

Over the years what has evolved is our timeframe. Now we prefer to do lunches, dinners, or cocktails. Typically, we do the Barn Raisings in someone's home. Then it's a much more relaxed environment. That's where trust continues to develop. Twenty-five years later we still answer the 3 questions, what's new, what do I have to give, what do I need? We've had a lot of different governance along the way but we've looped back to that. That's as simple as it needs to be. Then we do networking and see each other socially and business-wise.

My other groups I've had a once a month luncheon. This works better for the executive mothers. We tend to talk more about children and issues involved in raising a family, e.g., education, academic focused, college selection process, young adults launching careers, raising financially aware children, raising philanthropy focused good kids.

There's no better referral source than a Mastermind Group because all of the introductions will be high-quality and the probability of closing them is going to be dramatically higher. These referrals are going to be a great fit because the members of this group know you the best. Every person in your group is going to have very high credibility. These are the best of the best. And like a good wine, this will just get better over the years.

Alissa again:

Not everyone in the group has become a client as a result, but it has been a wonderful referral source. The client we just met with was a referral of one of the women in this group. That woman is not a big client but the client she referred us to is huge. We have kept tabs on all the ways we've gotten these clients. It's been a good and effective strategy. That's the reason we continue to do it. It's not just the personal connections; it's for business development.

This is a great idea for everyone. I've seen women really excel with these groups, and in my experience, men

could learn something from them. This is an excellent
way to make deep friendships, but it can be hard for
people because they're so busy. It's not golf; you really get
a chance to share business challenges with each other and
help each other to solve them and create that third mind.

Now these groups don't need to be exclusively female.
Alissa tells us of her business partner who started one called the
"Lunch Club," which is for both men and women. She says that
it has been very good for developing professional relationships.

An essential element is this.

Alissa explains:

> Carol and I are very selective about who we choose to bring
> into these groups. You want people who are like-minded
> with positive energy and a positive attitude about helping
> each other build their businesses. If there's not that collab-
> orative process, I don't think it works.

There are a variety of ways to organize your group, but
the constants I've found that balance everything are structure,
leadership, people willing to share their goals and their obsta-
cles to reaching those goals, a confidential climate, and an
85% attendance minimum. You should also have unanimous
acceptance of new members, and you have to be consistent
about firing people. That doesn't mean that that person can't
continue to be a friend or a COI but they just can't be part of
the Mastermind Group.

**While you need to own this group, you don't need to run it.
Make sure the president is doing their job.**

You could have rotating presidents every two years or have
a permanent facilitator. Either way, you always need to be ready
to run it if something goes wrong.

Next, there should be structure for each meeting and this
will happen by preparing an agenda. Each member talks for
five minutes, and then you to the hot-seat rotation for each
session. One person would really get into their story and their
challenges. Everyone then peppers you with questions until you

find a solution. You can even send out an executive summary which would include goals and responsibilities for follow up at the end of each meeting.

Now this won't always be easy. Alissa says it perfectly:

> In some cases, it's a thankless job continuing to keep my group together, but every time I do they walk away saying that was such a great session and thank me for keeping us going. We're all very busy women and it's hard to make a commitment. I look at it as making a commitment to each other. I had a recent experience where I had a health issue and I needed to call on these women, and it was very significant how much help they were to me personally. As a result, I realize the power of networks is not only professional, it is personal. It can be very impactful in your life. From that perspective, it helped save my life.

Now as we've shown, these groups are incredibly helpful both professionally and personally.

Don't let lack of time or shyness be a barrier to entry to a Mastermind Group. Alissa suggested an idea and I think that it's a great one:

> A Mastermind Group is not the end-all, be-all, but it's so helpful. I think you have to be willing to have a plan, stick to the plan, and be willing to get out of your own comfort zone to try something new. If that isn't your personality, you may want to create a group around one of your hobbies. For example, maybe you are part of horse club or a sailing club, maybe you race cars or are a supporter of the philharmonic? That might be a great way to find like-minded people who might want to be part of a group but don't necessarily want to start one themselves.

I've been frustrated by the difficult time most financial advisors have in adopting the Mastermind Group. I truly believe in it. I've seen it work. It is a way of developing a tremendous network that will benefit the financial advisors over time. It's something that takes infinite patience and most financial advisors haven't historically had that kind of patience.

Bill Cates on Mastermind Groups

My friend Bill Cates, author of numerous books and an expert in acquisition, affirms the benefits of developing a Mastermind Group:

> There are a couple overarching principles that are always guiding for me around this that I think are important to talk about.
>
> **First**, the concept of the mastermind is that third mind. It's hard to solve problems and come up with solutions in a vacuum. It can happen sometimes. Sometimes just walking down the road we have an "ah ha moment." What I've learned is that if we have a problem, an issue, there's a good chance there are other people who've had the same problem, same issue. We just need to find out who they are and we need to tap into that. That's the power of broad networking and making sure we know a lot of people in our industry and outside of our industry as well. We get an industry-think sometimes that we have to be careful about. For me, I have three Mastermind Groups. One group I've had for a long time.
>
> **Second**, the whole idea is to share an idea, something that's working. We have different agendas different times it seems, but the basic principle in most meetings is to bring an idea that's working for us that we share with others. We talk to each other and review each other about that idea. How can I make that idea apply to my business? Sometimes someone will say X and it triggers Y in our brain. We don't know why it triggers another idea. It relates somehow and we make that investment in time worthwhile.
>
> **Third**, we bring a challenge. One of the keys of a good functional Mastermind Group is the willingness to put our ego at the door and not try to be there to impress everybody and to come with a challenge.

Fourth, come a little bit of vulnerability and be willing to take on other thinking and not "pooh-pooh" somebody's idea too quickly. One of the things I've also learned that's helped me with the mastermind is that if somebody is having success with something—let's say they're doing Supernova. I see someone's having success with Supernova but I can't seem to make it work. I'm struggling to making this happen. What's the difference in George having success and me not? It's my beliefs, my belief system. I've got a limited belief; a mistaken assumption somewhere along the way that's keeping me from somehow engaging in a process that other people have proven to work. That's the mindset we need to bring to the Mastermind. We have limiting thinking.

Fifth, we have blind spots. One guy in my Mastermind Group calls it a scotoma (that's the medical word for a blind spot). Another guy says, "it's hard to see the picture when you're in the frame." It's the value over time of these other people that builds these trusting relationships where you know each member of the group has your best interest at heart. Any kind of critique, constructive criticism or questioning of your assumptions is coming from the place of wanting you to be successful. That takes time to develop. Time is a critical element. Then we can start to see those blind spots that maybe we kind of sensed were there but didn't really know. We don't know what we don't know. That's one of the powers of the groups, to find those blind spots and dissolve those things away for each other. Pretty much every Mastermind Group I've gotten into has started purely on the business level, but has always gotten to the point where we started to talk about other stuff in our life. It's all blended anyway.

Sixth, some incredible friendships build from these things as well. I have one group, we meet quarterly for a full day; we used to meet monthly; we're local. I have two other groups that meet twice a year and we're in different parts of the country so we rotate around where we meet.

Those usually are day-and-a-half meetings to get a lot of good work done.

Whenever someone thinks they're the smartest person in the room, they always discount the advice from other people. There are probably some people reading this nodding their head because they know somebody like that. Other people are wondering if they suffer from that phenomenon. You have to all be committed to each other's growth. You have to be committed to leaving your ego aside and not trying to impress each other. Some of that slips in, I get that. We're sharing wins with each other, but it has to come from that place of caring about helping the other person and also looking to get help.

CHALLENGE

Create a Mastermind Group! If you are having trouble getting busy people who would be a good fit to commit, try building the group with an escape valve. Do it for a 90-day free trial. The people who like it and see the benefits will see that in 90 days. Those who aren't comfortable can bail out.

NOTE

1. https://www.thehenryford.org/collections-and-research/digital-resources/popular-topics/the-vagabonds/
   http://www.businessinsider.com/andrew-carnegie-master-mind-principle-2015-6
   http://www.thesuccessalliance.com/what-is-a-mastermind-group/
   http://masterminds.org/the-5-most-popular-mastermind-groups-of-all-time/

CHAPTER

8

Niche Mastermind Groups—A Radical Idea

The Niche Mastermind idea can be likened to a Reese's—when two good things blend together, something great comes of it. Combining chocolate and peanut butter in a bite was brilliant. Tying a Niche with a Mastermind Group is, well, effective and efficient.

So how did these two forces come together? I was coaching an FA who wanted to know more about creating a Mastermind Group. We went over the who, why, what, and how of a Mastermind Group, and he was on his way. He went to his CPA to say he was setting up a Mastermind Group and ask if the CPA would like to join.

The CPA declined the invitation but offered for the FA to join his group. The CPA went on, "We have a group focused on helping physicians sell their practices to hospitals." In the group were a realtor, a business broker, a CPA to do the business valuation, and an attorney to write up legal documents. The only one needed to complete their Mastermind Group was a financial person to deal with the proceeds of these business sales. The CPA offered that the average sale was $5 million.

The FA was thrilled! He couldn't wait to tell me all about it. He said joining the group wouldn't have happened if he hadn't asked the CPA about the Mastermind Group. Then it struck me: this whole group was a Mastermind Group focused on a niche! What a great idea! This was the first time I had ever seen the two strategies put together to complement each other. It was a great marketing and service breakthrough and I chose to formalize it to add to my coaching tool-belt.

Where do you start? Mastermind or Niche? Start with the niche and build from there. Once you have identified your niches you can begin to build upon them by putting together a focused Mastermind Group for each niche. In identifying and inviting your core members, you can define it as a group of professionals who serve the specialized needs of a subset of clients. Examples of this would be a small business who is looking to sell or a group of doctors who are selling themselves to a hospital. Your Niche Mastermind Group might include all the specialties needed to serve the client who is selling their business. It consists of a business broker to auction off the group to the highest bidder, a lawyer to draw up the papers, a CPA to take care of the taxes, an FA to do the planning and investing, and a realtor to sell the building. This would be your core group, adding specialties as needed. For your clients, the group can be a think-tank and premier business concierge rolled into one.

What Exactly is a Mastermind Niche?

While a Mastermind Group is a general group of professionals in your community with whom you can exchange introductions, a Niche Mastermind Group takes it to the next level of introductions because it is a group focused on one niche. When you meet monthly, between meetings, you stay in communication via a message board or email listserv (e.g. Google+ Groups for an email list, Google+ Community or private LinkedIn Group). This forms the hub for (private) group communication. This is especially important if you all live in different parts of the country.

Virtually any niche can have a Mastermind Group serving it! You could create a niche for public companies such as Roche, Lilly, Abbott, Proctor and Gamble, UPS. When I was looking to sell a small company I was introduced to Mike Rasor, a local CPA, to discuss the selling of a friend's small business. He started the meeting telling me about his group that helps with the sale of businesses. He had a similar group to the previous story, plus two consultants that help people get ready for the sale of their businesses (they help clean up businesses to make them as attractive and profitable as they should be before they put them on the market). They have a CPA, attorney, financial advisor, and business broker. After hearing Mike's story, I decided to add this to my coaching sessions. I believe every team should have a Mastermind Group devoted to helping small businesses with their liquidity event.

Back to our friend Ken Shapiro who developed a Niche Mastermind Group focused on entrepreneurs:

> About 10 years ago I started the Strategic Advisory Board which was modeled after the YPO (Young President's Organization) forum.
>
> My group consisted of 10 individuals I chose. Each person runs their firm or a group in their business or they have a legal practice for a good-sized middle market. We meet every month for $1\frac{1}{2}$ hours for breakfast at one of our offices. Members make at least 80% of the meetings which is essential for the group dynamics. We talk about what's going on in our industry, what's going on in our lives, what client problems we need to solve and so forth. There is usually one person in the group that can really help us solve particular issues or use their experience to tell us how to get smarter. This works very well if, for example, I'm going to go speak somewhere and I need to know what's happening in the legal world, the tax world, etc.
>
> Then we also do events together both with spouse and family or just the group. The events that are just for us help us to be closer as a group. And that closeness translates into trust and confidence in each other. We go to the US Open every year and spend the first day together. We go to the Big East tournament for basketball every year and just go watch basketball in the afternoon and get lunch. We do a holiday dinner somewhere local. We also do client-focused prospect events. We also do three to four dinners a year

where we each invite a couple of our group as guest speakers at a Morton's. The idea is to have some fun times with interesting people that have commonalities that could be useful to them in the future including the guys in the group and the people the group members are inviting who are like them. We're inviting guests to the US Open this year. That group's been together for a long time. It's led to a lot of our best referrals with portfolios of $20–$50 million in assets.

Ken continued:

The industries represented on the board cross the spectrum but they are all service professionals. If you're a CEO of a company, what are all the things that have a high impact on your potential success from a business services perspective? You need to hire great people so you need a great executive search firm, you need to deal with your accounting personally so you need a great CPA. We tried having some private equity professionals in the group but we've found if you get a person in a principal capacity vs. professional services/advisory capacity, it's a conflict of interest because they tend to join to get first dibs at making a low-ball offer for buying the company. I can't introduce you to a buyer in good faith if I know he wants to get a deal from you below market. We ended kicking those people out of the group. Other than that, there is not much turnover.

Another guy was what I call a "black hole." You'd refer someone to him and he would never refer back. He had a great title and worked for a great company but was non-trusting, non-giving and the wrong personality. We replaced him.

Adam Grant in his book *Give and Take* refers to these folks as takers. They can pretend to be givers, but in the end, they are only interested in themselves. They have no place in your Mastermind Group. I always recommend you list what the

expectations of the group are. You want to address attendance, contributions, privacy of the information, and what is
acceptable and expected.

Ken did just that:

> We put together a contract everyone signs saying we'll
> attend most of the meetings and make a commitment
> to the group. This gave us the leverage to say "you're
> not cutting the mustard" if someone slacks off. Having
> a group with a lot of great referrals, great friendships,
> partnerships, is kind of unusual—and that's what makes
> them so effective. We met with a guy yesterday who had
> a question about moving his business from FL to NY. We
> talked to him about the tax consequences and becoming
> beholden to NY capital gains tax. After the meeting, I shot
> an e-mail to one of the top trust estate attorneys in NY
> who is actually not part of this group but we work with him
> like he is. Within ten minutes he came back to me with an
> answer for the client about what he should think about
> doing. This guy's pretty booked, but for us, he makes time
> because we bring him a lot of business.

If you could put together your "dream team" to attack a
niche what would it look like? For example, if you were wanting
to prospect retirement communities, who would you want on
your team? I would incorporate on this Mastermind Niche
dream team an end-of-life planning expert, an attorney specializing in estate planning, the CEO of the physicians group
that serves the elder community, an accountant, an investment
banker who specializes in this market, a CEO of Outsourcing
rehab company, a travel concierge planner, and the CEO of an
area hospital. Not only could your team service the needs of the
residents of this niche but you could also introduce each other
to all the qualified retirement communities in your market.

Let's take this a step further.

If you had a niche at an aerospace company such as Boeing you could put together a group that works in that industry
including an automation specialty company, an architect who

designs buildings for Boeing, the relocation expert for Boeing, a former Naval admiral involved in aerospace, a retired airline CEO, and the CEO of Boeing's metal refinishing provider. You could be the benefits and planning expert for the executive suite. Your group of experts would all be able to address all aspects of the business and problem solve for each other.

Back to Ken:

> We have another group we created in 2002 and consisted of more normal non-tech-related businesses—advertising, manufacturing company, retailer, distribution company, professional services company. We realized a lot of our clients, because of our backgrounds, come from the tech world in NY. We created this group to service this sector and called it the Media and Technology Advisory Group. The same kind of buckets we filled with people from different companies with almost an exclusive focus on technology companies. People are a lot more committed in this group and we've been strict about membership. To get in you have to meet everyone in the group. If anyone rejects you, you're dead. It's like an interview process. We tell them it's a probationary membership. After the first three months, we'll make it more formal.

After coaching people like Ken I knew I was on to something huge. Now Niche Mastermind Groups are an integral part of my coaching. Do note the distinction: this type of Mastermind Group doesn't necessarily include only your COI in the niche. You choose members who provide services to the niche and then work with their COIs and your COIs to find prospects who will need your "team's services." With each of you having COIs in the niche you will be able to find and serve clients efficiently, and more quickly than you ever could trying to do it alone.

What differentiates a Niche Mastermind Group from enthusiastically endorsed COI providers? Your Mastermind Group participants are going to bond and connect and trust each other at a deeper level. You will probably become good friends. There is an implied (or written) acknowledged code of conduct addressing confidentiality or nondisclosure. There will be an appointed leader who will do outreach to prospective members and create a means for group members to communicate. They will choose a meeting place and time and remind the others. You may require members to contribute into a common money pool that is used to cover everything from administration to the facilities for the group meetings. If you have a formal name it may require registering at state level. To lay the groundwork for a successful group, have clear communication channels, established membership processes for both joining and removal, and expectations—confidentiality; attendance; participation; contribution of ideas, introductions, and financial—defined and delineated.

Author and President of Referral Coach International, Bill Cates advises:

> It comes down to equal or roughly equal commitment, of course, from everybody in the group. You have to make sure people get value because if they're not getting value, they don't see the importance in spending or investing the time in travel or meetings. It also takes strong leadership. For two of the three groups I'm in now (I started one with another guy), I led the group for three years. Then I said I'm taking a step back and someone else has to lead. It really took me driving that for a little while.
>
> It's not a lot of work, but you just have to pay attention. You're herding the cats to get on that phone call or schedule the next meeting. Then we rotate the leadership. With one group, after the first meeting I said, all right, who's going to lead the next meeting? No one wanted to step forward. I said, look guys I'll take it on for the next meeting but after that, someone else has to take it on. What we've done with that group, whoever's place we're meeting at, in this case we're going to different cities/states, that person becomes the leader to kind of organize the next meeting and create the agenda for that meeting and be the one to keep the meeting going.

Some people are great at leading a meeting and some people are terrible. You just suffer through that and help each other out. As a team member, mastermind member, it's your job to make sure the leader doesn't fail. It's their job to make sure they don't fail but it's your job to help them. A lot of good stuff comes out for that as well.

For independent, fee-based fiduciary advisors this is an even more powerful concept. You may also want to consider an all-advisor group consisting of other RIAs. This is best done with people who don't live in the same territory and are not in direct competition with each other. You meet to discuss business, technology, planning, content, and strategies. Agendas may vary by format but typically involve one or several business/career/client challenges for the group to share and get candid feedback and constructive criticism from the group. For FAs who are the second generation in the business you would have a unique perspective and willingness to share openly about business and family planning issues that are crucial to your development.

My friend and Supernova advocate Rod, formed a close-knit group of his peers that has worked very well for him. The original group consists of FAs from the same firm who didn't compete with each other. In the last ten years, with some FAs retiring and new FAs (recommended by the retiring ones) joining, he now has 12 members who work in different markets and meet once a year.

We've all been in business for 25 years or more, we have similar work ethics, we are all loyal to the company, we are pretty good producers with production ranging from 2–4M. We now have an FA in Boston, an FA in Fort Worth TX, an FA in Las Vegas. Everyone in the group is either part of the original 8 or was recommended by someone in the group. We meet once a year to share ideas and experiences, problem-solve and exchange advice. This has provided me with a great resource and unlimited access to ideas I wouldn't have had otherwise. The group's based on a foundation of reciprocity, trust, respect and non-competition with each other.

Spending time together with like-minded individuals like this is a tremendous advantage. We usually start with dinner on a Thursday night, work all day Friday and finish at noon on Saturday. We invite spouses and they join us for the dinners. Sometimes we do social things but we also work really hard. We have a retired FA who used to be in the group who volunteered to be what we call the "master of ceremonies" and he runs the meeting for us. Everyone is assigned a topic to present to the group and it's put on the agenda for the meeting. Sometimes we will have two or more present the same topic but from different perspectives. I know it sounds intense, but we have found through trial and error that if it isn't intense these FAs won't come. We are busy people so taking this time away from our practices means this meeting has to be productive for each of us. Over time we have agreed to meet at least once a year. When we meet we discuss pressing issues in our industry and our firm. I know enough about the practices of the other FAs that if I have a question about something I know who to call. When you have that kind of access and trust you can pick up the phone and talk to any of them.

Back to Bill Cates:

I've developed a better sales process from working with some of the folks in the room. All kinds of stuff has come over the years from these folks. Occasionally, I've had business referred my way and vice versa. With advisors, if you have different specialties, or if you have a mastermind that isn't all financial advisors, then the opportunity for referral business is there. I couldn't imagine trying to build my business and growing in a vacuum. Not just from other people in my business. Other people have different business models, certain principles of business. Most financial advisors, generally speaking, aren't always great business people. They're good enough, but they're not as good as they could be. Being exposed to other great business people really makes a difference.

I think people go into Mastermind Groups thinking they can get a lot of introductions. What Bill knows, and what most people who are in successful groups have discovered, is that introductions are a potential benefit but shouldn't be the primary reason for forming a group. Rod's Mastermind Group, while not intended for potential client introductions, offers a wealth of intellectual capital, industry experience, and camaraderie to its members.

Mastermind Groups also offer some poaching protection. What you don't want is your client needing a service—legal, tax, real estate, etc.—and being pulled away from you while they are searching for that help by getting tangled in the web of another FA's Mastermind Group.

CHALLENGE

1. Form a group of professionals to service a niche.
2. Identify the niche.
3. Identify who would be a good fit.
4. Identify among those who are a good fit who would bring their energy to the group.
5. Set up the group and give it one year to see if you can function as a unit.
6. Use the 90-day Free Look Model if you need to get the group jump started. Don't wait for perfect. Get started now!

CHAPTER 9

Giving to Give

What does your volunteer involvement look like? How are you giving back to your community? You may be volunteering in a Big Brothers/Big Sisters program, serving on your local school/arts council/museum/scouts board, or on a committee at your church or place of worship. If you come from a medical background it might be the local hospital board, the American Cancer Society, or Little Red Door. If you belong to a charitable group, fraternity, or non-profit, and serve on their board in a leadership capacity, you are involved in the community.

We don't need a reason to give—we just do it because we know it's the right thing to do. It is natural to want to help each other be safe, successful, and happy. As author Adam Grant discovered in his research for his book *Give and Take*, the world is made up of three kinds of people: givers, takers, and matchers. Grant asserts that all three types can be successful but the givers are the most successful (and the happiest). "Being part of a group with shared interests, identities, goals, values, skills, characteristics, or experiences gives us a sense of connection and belonging. At the same time, being part of a group that is clearly distinct from other groups gives us a sense of uniqueness."

Becoming known and trusted in your community is necessary if you want to do business in that market. In fact, community involvement makes you into a marketing magnet. At no point do you actually ask for business. It will come to you naturally as you develop your connectivity with the community. You, as a successful person in the community, probably feel an obligation to give back and fulfill your civic responsibility. However, only a small portion of financial advisors are involved in a volunteer position in their communities and even fewer are very good at using their non-profit work as a marketing opportunity.

What does community involvement do for you?

- It gives you an opportunity to interact—as a peer—with the wealthiest and most powerful people in your community.
- It helps you broaden your network of contacts.
- It gives your life (and possibly your family's) meaning and fulfillment.
- It teaches your children social responsibility and exposes them to worthwhile causes, e.g. food banks, libraries, literacy initiatives, the arts.
- It is an opportunity to make life-long friendships.

Over the years I have observed that some FAs are very accomplished with social prospecting while the majority are rarely successful. What makes the difference? I found that there are distinct steps that the successful financial advisors take within their community. Most are oblivious to the fact that they are engaged in a process! They are unconsciously competent. They know it worked but they don't necessarily connect the dots.

In talking to one FA—the daughter of the founder of a regional brokerage firm, who is very involved in her community—I asked, "What percentage of your practice comes from your community involvement?" She said, "I don't know; I have never thought about it." It turned out that 30% of her clients came from the local boards on which she serves. We continued talking. I asked her if she had a plan for her community involvement.

She said, "No, I just have always been involved and feel it is a part of my civic responsibility." I then asked her how she manages her time and energy commitment to this effort. "I am on two boards at a time. Once I join a board I become involved on a committee that interests me, then I become the head of that committee, then vice president of the board, then president. After several years, I rotate off and join another board."

I asked her, "How long does that usually take?"

She responded, "Five to seven years. I have served on pretty much all of the boards in our community."

Never had anyone explained it so well and she didn't even know what she'd done! Most people join a board, and typically, don't really get involved. They arrive to meetings late and leave early. Then they lament: "I haven't gotten one lead, what should I do?" I explain that they haven't earned it. They haven't made an investment—of their time and talent—and can't expect any returns. It is a net-negative to belong to a board and not contribute. Such behavior is the recipe for a lackluster reputation at best. Padding your resumé or reputation is needed to fill empty spots and cover shortcomings. Fluffing your reputation with a disingenuous association with a charity screams poor character. Above all, you must be honorable if you want to be asked and tasked to handle someone's money—the money to educate their children, fund their retirement, support their charitable interests. You need to be seen as a leader, someone they can trust.

A Merrill Lynch team led by Ted Boots were early adopters of the Supernova Model and quickly reduced their client base from over eight hundred households in the year 2000 to less than three hundred by late 2001. As we continued our coaching engagement they were finding more time to prospect but also finding that their time-tested, original method of cold-calling had become less effective. The relatively new "do not call list" and the new practice at that time of prospects having only mobile phones made introductions via cold-call much less probable. I suggested that they wholeheartedly embrace social prospecting by actively contributing time and treasure to at least three organizations that aligned with their personal values. One of the FAs, Trent, joined a civic service organization and became chair of one of their major annual events, which had been going since the 1950s, while volunteering and becoming involved at the leading local children's hospital. Another

FA joined and immediately began helping plan a gala for a health-related non-profit, was elected to the board of the local club within a global civic service organization, and joined an advisory committee for one of the city's leading museums.

The goal was to meet Centers of Influence by becoming a Center of Influence, while tapping into their personal passion for serving the under-served. They found that demonstrating their commitment to the community led to stronger relationships with others in the groups and they quickly met leading influencers and wealthy prospects within the city. Within 18 months tangible rewards arrived in the form of new accounts, increased wallet-share of clients they had within the civic service organization, and more passion for work through their contributing to the betterment of their community.

By 2010 Trent became president of the civic service club; led the club through a strategic planning process that was closely followed by the launch of the civic organization's global headquarters; facilitated the rebuilding of their website; and led them to embrace digital communication. These all led to higher levels of member engagement. Importantly for their practice, he was able to begin working with several new households as well as the CFO of the global organization. This experience led him to being accepted into the city's premier fellowship of 25 emerging leaders, through which he met two consecutive state governors, and the CEOs of the city's three largest publicly traded companies, while still to this day building ongoing connections through the leadership group's alumni program. He is now on the board and executive committee of the city's symphony, on the finance committee of the art museum, on the board of a high-impact arts organization that focuses on community development, and serves as board chair of a missions-related organization. These activities provide a high "return on life" and meaning to the team's work. This has all led to business growth.

The long-term results of this effort are that 20% of the team's current households (32 out of 160 households) resulted from this initiative, with over $120 million in assets and $700k in production tracing directly back to this effort. Not only have the advisors' lives been enhanced through this involvement, but also their practice has significantly grown in terms of high-quality clients with whom they share common interests through involvement in the same organizations. This Merrill Lynch team has seen that alignment of social involvement with their values brings more joy to work while also bringing in more like-minded clients. They became people of influence within local leadership niches by volunteering and stepping up to lead in their community, their practice has grown, and targeted social prospecting in their case has borne much fruit.

Look at it the way this team did.

Every Minute You're on a Board, You're on a Job Interview

Be sure to join a board with the full intention of becoming president and making a significant contribution. Choose committees where you can be most effective. Do things that other people aren't willing to or can't do. As someone in the financial services industry, you have knowledge and a skill set which makes you a perfect candidate to join the finance or endowment committees and/or the development committee (fund raising). You must be willing to ask for money and raise money because that is what they need most. Other board volunteers will say, "I'm willing to do anything but ask for money." With your background and training, this is a golden opportunity for you to immediately create value on the board.

The person who asks for money can really help on the marketing and development committee. Your value to the charity can be to both fellow board members with what you bring and do at board level, as well as to the employees in the trenches. Being highly regarded by the key employees of the charity extends your circle. If you are their resource whenever they need a finance-related question answered, they will be additional ambassadors for your brand in the community. The particular committee is not as important as your earnest service to the non-profit. Join, get involved, contribute, be on a committee, become the head of that committee, then VP of the board, and then president for two years. From there you are forever a former president of that board with the benefits and status of that position.

Want to join a community or non-profit board? Here are the seven steps to follow:

1. Identify causes and organizations that interest you and you are passionate about.
2. Ask your clients for their advice on what board would be a good fit for you. Narrow your search to a couple of options.
3. Once you have two or three in mind, research them as you would any stock or fund. You will be investing your time, talent, and reputation with them for several years. If you aren't in it 100% the volunteers will sense your lack of passion for the cause and think of you as insincere. Then meet with the executive director of the organization or the head of the development or governance committee. Suggest a lunch where you get to know them and they get to know you and see if it is a good fit. Ask questions at this meeting to find out the time commitment, where the strengths and weaknesses are, and how you can best serve them. Read at least the last year's board minutes. Are they in good order? Are they filing the necessary reports and documents to maintain their non-profit status? Do they provide you with D & O insurance? It may be a worthy cause but a disaster in practice. You can't afford either your time or reputation in joining a dysfunctional board, associating with questionable or desperate financials, or taking on the day-to-day operations if the management is unstable or in crisis mode.
4. Before you agree to join the board attend a social event and get to know some of the board members. It has to be a good fit in both directions. You will likely need to pass a background check and be approved by the board.
5. Once on the board, after serving on a committee, volunteer to be the head of the committee (usually a two-year commitment).

6. After serving as head of a committee volunteer to be trea-
surer or vice president of the board. This will put you in line to
be president in two years.

7. Serve the two years as president then stay involved as the
past-president by continuing to sponsor an event and support the fundraising efforts and social activities.

The way you get elected president is by building up your
board constituency. Make friends. Meet with board members
outside of the committee and board meetings. Have dinners,
have fun. If they like you and trust you, they'll encourage you
to run for president. You probably won't even have to suggest
it because these boards need leadership. There are very few
people who are willing to be engaged. Remember, the more
prestigious the board, the more prestigious the position. When
you've demonstrated leadership and they like working with you,
then you'll have earned their business.

Nothing here is a shortcut. You may be recruited to the
board for a particular committee because of your forte, speed-
ing you along the road to presidency, but this is based on your
known success on other boards. There is no shortcut for this
process. Once you've done it once or twice, you will become
adept at it. When you get on a board where you already know
people, it will take you less time to run through all of those
positions. If you don't know people in your community, you
may have to start in a junior committee position, serve in a
different capacity, volunteer.

Most every advisor will have clients who are networked into
the community. This is a systematic process—go to your clients
and let them know that you have time "at this stage in your
career" and you've been thinking about actively giving back to
the community and ask which boards they suggest you consider.
They're going to have their own passions they will share with
you. Do your homework and be very appreciative of the introductions and help they offer. If an organization that was brought
to you by a client is on your shortlist ask them to arrange for

the two of you to meet with its director or board president. I did this when I joined the Indianapolis Opera. My friend, who recommended me for the board, arranged a lunch to meet the director. This turned into an invitation to be a board member. They were thrilled by my interest and capability in helping their board. Remember, you want to interview with several boards before you decide which one will be a good fit for you. Since this will be a seven-year commitment—do your homework!

When you are on Step Three of the board process and have your meeting with the director or board members ask specific questions such as:

- How healthy is the organization?
- How many committees are there?
- What is the expected additional time commitment at the committee level?
- What other professionals do you have on the board?
- Do you budget on expected grants and historical donor trends and cut back if they aren't realized?
- How does the board handle budget deficits?
- If there is a financial shortfall are you, as a board member, responsible to fill in the gap or do they "borrow" from any endowment?
- What is your process for raising money?

Your fiscal credibility will be tied to your board membership of this organization. You want to know who the current board members are; are they engaged in a capital campaign or is there any board member training available or expected? Can you tour their facilities or operations? What companies sponsor their efforts? Remember there is a pecking order of the most prestigious boards, and you will have to prove yourself before you have earned your seat at the table.

Consider joining one arts organization and one charitable organization. This way you strike a balance and cross-section of people. When I was a manager in Indianapolis, I served on the Indianapolis Opera board. This was an organization I was passionate about. I was also on the board at a local Assisted Living facility. The combination worked well for me as I was passionate about both organizations. Serving on a board can give you great experiences in dealing with challenges and opportunities. Your business experience and financial expertise can be a big help to these organizations, who tend to be supported by well-meaning enthusiastic supporters of the cause with little or no business acumen.

Ideally you want to join organizations where you have a personal interest. These can become niches like the others, but you're much more involved because you're **on** the board and part of that community versus just an informed member of the public.

I also volunteered for Brooks Place, a non-profit that helps grieving children who have lost a loved one. Through the Y, I taught remedial English to children who were lagging behind. I have many wonderful memories of interacting with the kids and knowing I was making a difference.

Once you are accepted as a new member it's important you learn their terminology or language. You've got to understand the business end of the organization and the scope of their services. For the arts, what contribution do ticket sales make to the overall cost of running the opera, museum, ballet, or orchestra? Will you also be expected to support events by purchasing a table or sponsorships? If so, it may be possible to take those funds from your marketing budget. If you are working for a large wire house you can also approach your branch manager to have everyone from your branch get involved or for the branch to be a corporate sponsor for an event.

He Found His Niche in What He Loved to Do

In Chapter 6 we discussed Patrick Renn who found his niche based on his passion. It is worth reiterating some of his thoughts.

I was always interested in charitable planning for my clients. Over the years I have served on many nonprofit boards and thought it was very fulfilling to help these charities build their endowment to meet their day-to-day expenses.

One year I was involved in Special Olympics. We secured some sponsors but were still looking for more. One of them introduced me to a guy who was very interested in helping us. He owned multiple retail locations of a well-known brand and was very generous to the cause.

Years later, when he decided to sell his company, he called me to see if I could help him with the sale. I prepared to make a pitch to manage his assets and he just looked at me and said, "I'm not one to get involved in all the nitty gritty details, you have the reputation of being able to handle this kind of thing so just give me the forms and I will turn it all over to you."

Having this kind of a reputation is worth more than a big office, fancy stationary, or having multiple accreditations. Don't get me wrong, all of those things are nice, but your reputation in the community, in a niche, will help you grow a successful business.

I wasn't looking for anything more than to help a cause I was interested in. It turned out I was very good at what I did and my reputation spoke for itself. I think when you show people who you are, they will be naturally attracted to that and want to do business with you.

Building Personal Relationships

In order to get elected president of a board or eventually be trusted with introductions, you must build personal relationships along the way. For example, you could take the initiative and say to another board member, "Let's get together and have lunch." Spend the first half of the meeting asking about them.

Ask about family, business, hobbies, and other interests. Ask them about their firm. You might say, "What does your ideal client look like? What is your firm's specialty?" Show interest and let them talk. Eventually they will want to know more about you.

Alissa Quinn (you remember her from Chapter 7) discussed her team's commitment to giving back, social networking, and using her Mastermind Group in her community:

> For us, our presence in the community and giving back to our community is what it's all about. My business partner and I have won a number of professional accolades/awards. Last year Carol won the award for Women of Excellence Through Sales & Marketing in the Albany Chamber of Commerce. I had won Trailblazing Woman of the Year Award through our local community foundation which is based on philanthropy and leadership.
>
> Carol and I are extremely involved in the not-for-profit community. We're utilizing all our professional connections within these groups to continue to network so we are very, very active out in the business community. We support the women's employment resource center, which allows women to get re-trained and back in the workplace.
>
> We annually participate in a huge luncheon benefitting the American Heart Association. We're actively involved with the American Cancer Society and Girls Inc. (an organization that supports inner city girls to be strong, smart and bold). We have some charitable organizations where we are actively involved. We now have a focus on setting up donor advise funds for our client base. I just opened my own Quinn Charitable Family Fund. That's a whole new avenue of giving.

Another example of a financial advisor who gave back with no expectations is my friend, Rick Rogers. Rick is involved on a number of church-related boards. He started on the Finance

Council for his church, progressed to the Pastoral Council, and then was asked to serve on the board for an affiliated group. He provided a steady, prudent but strategic hand in the management of their endowment. When it came time to interview for a new consultant for their endowment two board members went directly to the leadership committee and recommended Rick. He agreed to serve as their consultant, resigned from the board, and has been helping them ever since.

Rick's story:

> I just happen to be involved in a lot of religious boards. One of the boards I served on for many years had an outside consultant they had used forever. The consultant wasn't as sharp as we wanted so the board decided to open a new search to replace him. Unbeknownst to me, other board members went to the president, and questioned why they should do a search when they already had someone on our board that is known and trusted. It was suggested to just give me the opportunity. It was decided to not do a search, and when they asked me if I would be interested in making a presentation to them I jumped at the chance. For my exposition to the committee, I brought in one of our institutional consulting teams to show how deep my bench is and the resources that I bring to the table. Even though I didn't need the backup, I wanted to have it because I think it showed appropriate respect or homage to the opportunity they were giving me. We ended up bringing in that $60 million account.

In conclusion, it is easy to ignore this aspect of asset acquisition. You might feel like you should be at your office talking to clients rather than sitting in a room with a group of people deciding what operas to schedule for next year or how to expand the kids' summer free lunch program. It's all important. Time given to your community is time well spent. Especially if it is a cause you believe in.

CHALLENGE

1. Make a commitment to have your team become established and trusted in your community. Each teammate should: join two boards and donate their time, talent, and resources to helping the organization reach its fullest potential.
2. Encourage your spouse to do the same.
3. Be "otherish" in your commitment with the strategies outlined in this chapter.
4. Follow the seven-step process to successful board experiences.

CHAPTER

10

Leveraging Social Media

Whether you like it or not social media should be an essential part of every advisor's practice. There are a myriad of uses you can find for the various outlets and applications available to your practice. These are limited only by your interest, skill, time, and the safeguards and regulations that apply to our industry. Social media currently encompasses the available online communication channels designed for community and business-based sharing of content and for communication, interaction, and collaborative use.

I see three reasons for using social media. The first one is the opportunity to "give" to your clients, your community, and your industry. Your insights about the markets, your wisdom on how to help clients, and your ability to verbalize and comment on information that may be confusing for the outsider is a gift you can share without any assumption of a return. If just one person is better informed about the issues around retirement, interest rates, debt, etc., you can be assured you have done your job as a giver. The second reason is the opportunity to get to know your existing clients at a deeper level by engaging with them on one of these platforms. The third is to acquire prospective clients through social media introductions. Some of the most-used platforms are LinkedIn, Twitter, Instagram, Google+, Pinterest, and Facebook. You may also have your official team (corporate) or personal website to consider when thinking about social media opportunities for your practice. However, keep in mind you will have compliance regulations to consider whether you are associated with a firm or are an independent advisor.

According to a recent survey by Putnam Investments,[1] 85% of financial advisors use social media for business. Eighty percent of these "social advisors" gained new clients resulting in nearly $5 million in average asset gain directly attributable to social media use. Also, 85% said social media shortened the selling cycle. For these advisors, social media is no longer an option but is a proven tool used to gain new business and to build closer relationships with clients.

Back to our friend, Alissa Quinn:

> Many of us in our industry are more seasoned professionals that didn't grow up with this technology. I think it's just a mindset. I'm still shocked that very few FAs are utilizing this media. They're not connecting the dots. Lots of people are on LinkedIn or Facebook, but they're not using it to connect and strengthen their relationships and deepening trust.
>
> For us, that is the reason to be using these mediums. Some FAs are looking at it as "I'm not going to waste my time doing that." It can be a black hole where you can spend a tremendous amount of time; you have to be very efficient, productive, strategic. There has to be a social media strategic plan as part of your business plan for it to be effective. I think people go to the low-hanging fruit and are so busy doing all their projects. I just finished our team meeting, and social media continues to be part of our discussion.
>
> I tell my team, "Every client who is on LinkedIn HAS to be a connection for us." That has to be a top priority. However, in the case of Facebook, we have to be a bit more selective and only connect with clients we have a strong personal connection with. It's not going to be every one of our clients.
>
> The times that I have connected with someone on Facebook, I know the glue is far more substantial than with us not having a connection. I would say if I feel

> comfortable adding a client to FB, it makes the
> relationship with that person far more powerful than with
> someone I am connected to on LinkedIn. We tend to use
> LinkedIn more for connecting with prospects and doing
> it professionally. FB is for those people in your life you are
> closer to and want to be.

As Alissa said, Facebook is a powerful tool for becoming
closer to existing clients and developing deeper relationships.
Consider having an active team Facebook profile and well as
individual profile. Your profile should focus on community
involvement and charitable activities. Use the pictures from
your community walks, bike rides, fundraisers as background
for your team pictures in the boardroom. You should post
your team's activities and a calendar of upcoming community
events that your team and you are attending, participating in,
or sponsoring.

Alissa continues,

> Facebook helps me understand more about my best clients
> and their families. The very nature of what you do makes
> you a public figure. The excuse "I don't want my name
> out there" or "I don't want to get involved with Facebook"
> is an indication your business model is outdated. What
> can you learn from connecting with your existing clients?
> A rapid understanding of their charitable interests, their
> family, and their activities. This information gives you
> an opportunity to have conversations that are more
> meaningful and accurate.
>
> I may not have had a conversation with someone in the
> last four years but when I do (and we are friends on social
> media) both of us feel like we know things about each other
> that have happened over that time and can discuss it. It just
> feels more natural and more relaxed. I feel flattered when
> someone keeps up with my posts and my life.
>
> When we're networking in the community we're
> networking with hundreds and hundreds of people.
> Again, we're connecting with LinkedIn and social media.

For example, I met with a client who moved to Florida. We had a 25-year relationship, but once you move away, you feel more distanced. He only wants to come in once a year; he doesn't want to do our Supernova process. We tried so hard to get him in four times, call him to touch base but he prefers only to do it once a year face to face. I'm on Facebook with him and the minute he walked in he said, "Congratulations, your son graduated from college. I can't believe your daughter is going there too. That's fantastic." That was all Facebook. He said it's not necessary to talk more often. The relationship is as personal as possible. We try, but there will be some avenues that don't work so you have to define what works. We find social media fills in the blanks when they don't want to have monthly meetings, or can't logistically, and keeps that trust going. That's all we use social media for, to maintain and deepen the trust and get to the next generation. On Facebook, we can see they're spending time with their grandchildren, the names of their grandchildren, how many, etc. You can't do that in regular review appointments when you're doing performance reviews, updating financial plans and educating them on a new service. Social media fills that trust band in a significant way if done discreetly and appropriately. We learn about significant events in their lives without being caught up in the minutiae of social media. That's a hole you can be sucked down.

My son did a term abroad when he was at Boston College. He went to Russia, India, China, Turkey, Israel, England, Germany. We knew he was becoming culturally enriched as we watched it unfold. He was comparing and contrasting global emerging markets around the world and doing it with an alumnae network. That's very powerful.

When I opened my first donor-advised fund, I put it on Facebook and said, "I just started the Quinn Family Charitable Funds as a result of two upcoming graduations." I'm using it as a way to encourage our young adults to live a life of philanthropy. They're getting in part for their graduations a gift certificate of giving, and they have to decide which charitable organizations they want to support and why. That will be a topic of discussion in our family.

I found this to be a way to connect with people who commented, "what a great gift/idea, you're empowering your children"—they're validating our family values. We're not posting the minutiae of the day, we're posting what's important to us and our kids foremost, but it is a way we're connecting with our clients. We have one client who has a child with Williams Syndrome. That's a fairly rare birth disorder. They're doing the Williams Walk. They're posting now on FB once a month an awareness of what Williams Syndrome is. That's a client I had never met in person, and it's the child of one of our wealthiest clients. They're in Pennsylvania, and they have small assets now but will inherit. We need to have those trusting relationships. Every year I donate to that Williams fund and the walk and cheer them on. It's using social media in a way to continue to connect with things that are important to our clients. Putting our pulse on that and supporting that every way we can. That's what going to continue to develop the trusting relationship we have.

As Alissa stated,

Knowing what your clients are passionate about makes the first ten minutes of your conversation during a review more meaningful to both of you. When your initial discussions during your reviews are more personal and intimate, you don't spend a tremendous amount of time getting caught up. Before I went into any review, I would look up my FB connection with them and bring myself up to date. We want people to know who we are and are very flattered by that attention.

Acquiring New Clients through LinkedIn

LinkedIn is your primary media outlet for communicating your team's premier financial services and brand in the business community as well as a resource for introductions. When someone does an internet search for your name, two things come up—your business website and your LinkedIn homepage.

Be sure that what they find is the best representation of your team and you. You have only one chance to make a good first impression. LinkedIn is your connection to the business, professional, academic, etc. world. It is considered today's way of advertising—so be sure everything looks professional including your pictures, profile, interests, others, and companies with whom you are linked. You should consider making a small investment in your team and in yourself by upgrading to a professional version of LinkedIn, and it should be well done and 100% complete. The technology for these sites changes randomly and often. Make it a priority for someone on your team to maintain your page and update the material at least quarterly to ensure it is accurate.

Once you have established your social media presence, make it a showcase for your brand that you are proud of. Use LinkedIn to connect to your immediate community as well as your larger circle of community and influence, e.g., former colleagues, friends, business associates, college friends, Community Board members, fellow volunteers, etc. As a general rule, If you are an active member of the LinkedIn community, you should have somewhere between 500 and 2,500 connections. It is necessary to regularly post articles of interest that are timely and of interest to your clients and prospects and that demonstrate your value and insight into your communities and/or the financial services industry. You want to be perceived as a thought leader for your community and industry. Make sure you have a clear understanding of your compliance obligations and restrictions prior to hitting the send or post button. Once you have a well-reviewed LinkedIn presence with a large number of followers you have a socially acceptable way of acquiring new introductions in your immediate community, as well as in your larger circles of community and influence.

Ken Shapiro:

> What we do a lot is, if we saw in the paper Rob Knapp sold his company for $40M to Thomson Financial, the 1st thing we do is find Rob Knapp's name on LinkedIn to see who we know who knows him. Start with clients, down to friends, then COIs. If three friends know Rob Knapp we'll call the friend and say, "I see you know Rob Knapp, do you know him well enough, you know what we're doing, this is how we could help him, could you make an intro, how could we do this?" We'll call the client and say the same thing. We want to grow our business.

My suggestion is to identify the people with whom you want to reconnect and who you think can directly do business with you or who may become Centers of Influence for you. Reach out to them or update your connections with them through LinkedIn's message app. This method has been successful for me on numerous occasions to identify potential new hires, partners, clients. Always follow up with a personal note when they agree to an invitation to connect with you or when they message you. Also, use LinkedIn's notification system of anniversaries, job changes, etc. as an opportunity to reach out to them. You never know when this may result in new business or new connections. One never tires of receiving congratulations, good news, or a quick "hello." When sending an invitation add a note as to who you are (either refreshing their memory or as a quick introduction) and why they might want to connect with you. That will give the other person a better understanding of who you are and will increase the likelihood of having the connection accepted.

As an example, I was fortunate to be contacted by a highly esteemed group of financial services professionals in Brazil via LinkedIn. This introduction resulted in a speaking engagement at XP Investimentos in San Paolo, Brazil. As the largest investment firm in Brazil, they make it their mission to find thought leaders in other countries who are willing to make presentations to them about the state of the industry that will educate and inspire their advisors; and they do this through their LinkedIn connections. If my LinkedIn presence wasn't highly visible or if I had ignored their request to connect, I doubt I would have been invited to speak at their national convention.

As a financial advisor, how could you further leverage the use of LinkedIn? I would first identify target niches, make connections to COIs within those niches, and expand your relationship with their LinkedIn friends and associates. This way, before any face-to-face meetings with that Center of Influence, you would already have a solid list of introductions you could suggest.

Consider creating a community on LinkedIn of business people with similar interests. Jason Macaluso is an FA who did this very early on and created quite a network of triathletes. This network resulted not only in more business but also close friendships. He attributes a great deal of his success to his business model, Triathlete Business Network on LinkedIn, with 5,408 members. Being a triathlete himself, Jason felt there wasn't a forum for triathletes to share ideas on the sport as a profession or just a way for weekend athletes to share their experiences. He was able to convince his firm that it was a good idea and it turns out he was right. He has connected to dozens of fellow business athletes who have become friends and clients. The key for Jason or anyone considering doing this is a genuine interest in the group. Your primary motivation must be to help connect people and to solve problems. You could do this with any hobby or skill, from fly fishing to coaching kids in soccer. Take your passion and turn it into a tool to leverage your personal and business life for greater success and personal satisfaction in both areas.

As I said before, it's important to keep in mind compliance regulations. According to Joanne Belby, a compliance specialist for Proofpoint:[2]

> Based on your firm's social media policy, you may find that your firm has specific requirements for your social media profile. Many firms require setting up the account with your business email for recordkeeping purposes. Or when using LinkedIn as an example, firms typically prohibit "Recommendations" and "Skills and Endorsements" to

avoid the appearance of a testimonial. If so, and these already appear on your profile, you may be asked to "hide" them. For consistent firm branding, you may be instructed to include a pre-approved paragraph that describes your firm. Once your profile is complete, your firm may require it to be reviewed by a registered principal of the firm before publishing it in keeping with advertising rules of the industry.

She also says:

Many financial services firms have libraries of articles that have already been pre-approved by compliance that you may share on social media. Share the content that matches your brand, demonstrates your specific expertise and is of interest to your clients/followers. Be consistent. If allowed by your firm, personalize the message of content from the library so that it's in your voice. If permitted, also find and share additional articles that will be of interest to your clients and prospects. To make this less time consuming, you can set up alerts on Google for topics of interest. Blogging is also useful to establish your brand (albeit time consuming) and a way to demonstrate that you are an authority in your field. As with everything, check your firm's policy before proceeding.

What do you say when you are trying to connect on LinkedIn with the associates of one of your Centers of Influence? Your script should focus on what you are going to do for them and how you can be helpful. If you have expertise in a particular niche, you can mention what your qualifications are and what you will do to help them. For example, if your focus is on entrepreneurs in the artificial intelligence and robotic industry you can mention the fact that you have been an experienced entrepreneur in that area, and are willing to connect the person with others in the industry who can potentially create a benefit for both of you.

Social media provides powerful tools that every FA should use to understand their clients better and to connect with new business opportunities.

If you don't have an online presence now is the time to stop procrastinating. Start with your corporate team page. Have a professional team photo taken, list your credentials, mission statement, service commitment, and other market-related things you want to add. Take a look at Facebook and LinkedIn and notice how others in the industry are approaching social media. Create your Facebook and LinkedIn profiles. And don't forget to have someone on your team update your social media at least twice a year.

NOTES

1. https://www.putnam.com/advisor/business-building/social/
2. https://www.forbes.com/sites/joannabelbey/2017/01/03/financial-advisors-15-tips-to-use-social-media-compliantly/#55e76aff75d1

CHAPTER

11

Leveraging Debt to Your Client's Advantage

J ust as this book moves in two worlds—your actions and your mindset—it also connects two eras of Supernova practice. In 2007 Supernova launched, and the following period saw its first years of performance; the core elements were: extraordinary service, rapid response to problems, financial planning, intentional acquisition, and a highly efficient and effective organizational model. Deliberately absent was any language on any particular investment strategy.

In its infancy the Supernova Process was "investment model neutral." I assumed your investment strategy was brilliant. I assumed you are competent and accomplished in your financial advising career. I believed the teams I work with are financially literate, investment savvy, and well versed in market trends. I wasn't cheeky, but I also didn't want to get into a discussion on returns. I still don't. Assuming you are truly committed to growth I want you to do some deep thinking on an aspect of clients' financial lives that has been, at best, ignored, and at worst, demonized: DEBT. This is the proverbial elephant in the room.

If you are reading this book you are invested in planning and preparing for your Supernova practice of the future. You are defining what makes the practice you have now different from your competitors' practices. Your goal is to be superior. To best yourself and others you will need to be brilliant. You can stand out by being able to guide clients through an effective debt strategy, and when possible (and it's always possible) connecting them with the debt products that deliver on that strategy. For many clients, debt managed strategically will emerge as a defining characteristic of their own financial success, which will naturally reflect your Supernova practice.

The added facet of a debt strategy as another service of your practice enhances its value. Your investment strategy may be ingenious but it doesn't look any different from the 15 other teams that are calling on clients. Every advisor can generate impressive returns. Every advisor has a large-cap growth fund. Every advisor allocates against risk tolerance and time horizons.

But here's the real news: more and more firms and more and more teams have proven the original Supernova truth:

> Fewer clients served better equals higher production.

When Supernova was born, a smaller book was counter-intuitive, if not outright heresy. Today, it's conventional wisdom. And today, I believe debt has the counter-intuitive edge that will propel production faster and more consistently than any other single practice element. "Heresy!" you exclaim? OK, let's go there.

When It Comes to Debt, Words Matter

The words your clients and you use are critically important for understanding the strategic use of debt instruments. Unfortunately, and restrictively, most people's vocabulary on debt includes all of two words: "bad" or "necessary." I don't entirely disagree, but let's not stop at two, let's add "strategic" and even "enriching."

When you talk about it with your clients remember that you OWE them the opportunity to discuss debt. With this simple mnemonic acronym, you move it from hidden to happening. People often have an emotional reaction when they hear the word "debt." It's your job to bring it into the conversation, educate the client, and have it a part of their overall financial plan. In conversations with your clients, lift debt from taboo to topical.

Think of debt in three categories with the acronym OWE:

Oppressive Debt: Paying more than 10% interest is oppressive debt. Most credit card balances are oppressive debt. Plenty of people—including some of the high-net-worth (HNW) households you are advising and prospecting—have experienced oppressive debt. It's debilitating; it can be soul-crushing to the individual carrying the burden.

Working Debt: A mortgage at 4% or the equally low-interest-rate student loan would be considered working debt. It is money borrowed to acquire an appreciating asset that would otherwise be out of reach. This is an example of using debt as a tool. These "working debts" may also provide some tax advantages. Unfortunately, it's also the kind of debt that millions of people are paying down as if it's oppressive debt. In reality, working debt's bad rap is usually more about psychology than "fiscalology." It is more about how your clients view these debts than how the debts affect the clients' financial picture.

Enriching Debt: With this type of debt you are thinking and acting like a corporate CFO. You take on this debt by choice and can pay it off at your convenience. This kind of debt is strategic, and it creates possibilities for asset growth. Apple, one of the world's most valuable companies, is sitting on $257 billion in cash while choosing to have $148 billion in debt. Is the CFO an idiot? Of course not. Apple's CFO, like all true CFOs, value liquidity and flexibility.

O, W and E are the three flavors of debt, and just as your financial services and products are not a one-size-fits-all, neither is debt. For example, debt would be unnecessary for a retired client who needs less than 3% annually after tax from their portfolio. You probably advise clients like this all the time—they have a pension, and social security, and they live sensibly and always have.

But what about the client who needs more? If a client needs 4%, 5%, or 6% from their portfolio, they will have to take risks. That means strategic asset allocation or strategic debt. Both High-Risk asset allocation and taking on debt have a risk associated with them. Doesn't it make sense to choose the less risky option when faced with two types of risk? Strategic debt at 3% frees up dollars that can generate 5%. That's CFO thinking. And what about the client who needs 7% or more? You need to have debt management in your toolkit, period.

All of this makes a strong argument against one of the standard questions in any client introduction: "What's your tolerance for risk?" My answer: "Who cares?" A cardiologist doesn't ask you what's your tolerance for pain before treating you. They run the diagnostics, study the literature, and propose a treatment plan. My feelings, or my fears, reside only on the margins of the decision making—they are important; however, they don't drive the decisions. Advisors, especially Supernova advisors, can learn from that approach. Stop asking about risk tolerance (a feeling) and start working with the goals and the resources (the facts) that you already know.

Let's bring in Tom Anderson. Tom is an advisor, teacher, and author. His book *The Value of Debt*[1] takes these ideas and expands them exponentially. I highly recommend this book. I was honored to be invited to write the book's foreword and agreed immediately because I was impressed by his strategic approach to debt and what it offers both advisors and clients. I believe the work Tom has done in developing strategic debt strategies and guiding clients as they execute them opens up a powerful new pathway for Supernova advisors. Using Tom's debt strategies, you will accomplish two critical missions: 1) provide a valuable service, and 2) differentiate yourself from your competition.

Here's Tom:

> Debt is not the right approach for every client, but every single advisor should have a philosophy on debt that goes beyond "It's bad, pay it down." How are you going to develop that philosophy? My guess is you didn't learn

much about debt in undergrad or B School, or in your training. Just walking into work, you trip over equities strategies. Debt? You must become an expert yourself. And don't discount the instruments because you don't make a big number when you close one. Because if you don't close it, another institution will, and while they are working the application your clients will hear all kinds of sweet talk on discounts tied to assets with the bank. What's more, every one of those assets will be right there in the file—your statements, other assets, everything. You want to know what someone owns, have them fill out a loan application.

Debt strategies and products give advisors both an offensive and a defensive play. If you're taking the loan app it's you who sees the assets—all of them, right away—and you who can provide a discount with assets moved. But defense may be the most potent way to think about debt. Supernova does an amazing job of building a wall around your clients. A comprehensive debt strategy—especially around mortgages and credit lines puts a hardcover on your fort and gives you the comfort of knowing you may never lose another client again. Ever.

But he's just getting started. Let's talk taxes:

FAs have always said "I can't give tax advice. The sirens go off, and the compliance department swoops in." Not giving tax advice to a client that is retired, outside of pension and social security, is a problem because all their tax consequences are going to be driven by decisions you (the FA) make for them. You can help them with the timing of their minimum distribution from an IRA, RMDs, pensions and social security. And you can guide them in all other areas, for example, selling investments and triggering capital gains. When they need cash will you take out more from an IRA? You can keep track of what is the best solution.

I used to say, "we took $50K last time from the IRA; we need to take money from the taxable account this time."

You don't need to be a tax accountant, but you need to be highly conversant in tax facts. When you understand tax facts and deploy debt strategies you are essentially creating the future of wealth management—a comprehensive, integrated and holistic wealth management strategy means seeing assets, liabilities and taxes combined.

Wow. That is powerful. In the past, we've used "Chief Financial Officer" (CFO) as the role we want to serve for our clients, but by bringing tax and liabilities entirely under the tent, we've become the CFO for our clients. I don't believe the industry can turn back, and it certainly can't stay the same.

Tom again,

You're one of 300,000 financial advisors. Looking forward, is it possible you can say, my asset allocation model is better than yours; therefore, I can charge a 1% asset management fee? Am I better at picking ETFs than someone else? Sorry. That business is dead. Technology has made 60/40 and 50/50 asset allocation models essentially free. The future of wealth management is giving your clients honest and transparent value-added advice. Clients will pay for value, and there isn't any value in selecting the best 60/40 asset allocation fund. There's value to managing both sides of the balance sheet. There's value in making portfolio decisions with a clear eye on tax implications. Assets, liabilities, and taxes. That's where the future of wealth management is going.

What does that mean in real-world terms?

When I moved first to Chicago in 1979, interest rates on money funds were paying 22%, and long treasuries were paying 14%. Knowing that interest rates higher than 10% weren't sustainable, I told people that those 14% treasuries were a collector's item. I knew that interest rates higher than 10% were not sustainable. Today, we look back and realize that the inflation caused by the surge of the baby boomers through the system generated unsustainable growth and more inflation.

A personal story: my wife and I took out an adjustable rate mortgage on our new home (in 1979) because of my strong conviction about this economic probability. Mortgage rates on the short end were 10% and almost immediately went to 12%— it was an interest-only loan, six months adjustable, and I was paying 12%. As it continued to go up and my wife got more and more anxious, I assured her interest rates can't go past 22%. I didn't panic, and interest rates gradually began to decline steadily for the next 37 years. I haven't paid anything but interest on any of my houses ever, and I've consistently made money in the equity and bond markets because I had a strategic debt. I never had more leverage than I could pay off quickly, and I always had a contingency plan. I kept the same amount of money in bonds to offset the mortgage.

Will it always work? No. If we have sustained high inflation in a rising-interest-rate environment, it won't work. I always had the ability to pay off the debt if I needed to do it. I also knew that if the economy were so strong that interest rates were going up rapidly, the stock market would reflect the strong earning of America's companies and would make new highs. I ran my balance sheet like a business. I was truly the CFO of my own family money. And today, I can still make use of that money in so many better ways than paying off that mortgage. By the way, the houses did gradually appreciate along the way.

The recommendation here is not to suggest anyone go out and take on new debt to enhance a lifestyle. Instead, it is to have a thoughtful strategic plan using debt while maintaining a disciplined balance sheet. The goal is to manage your clients' liability risk as prudently and thoughtfully as you manage their asset risk.

CHALLENGE

Make asset/liability and risk management an integral part of your financial planning practice. Teach your clients how to look at the three kinds of debt, act as a CFO would, and get away from the black/white

(*continued*)

(*continued*)

or good/evil view of debt. Make liability management an agenda item on your regular 12-4-2 model. Set a realistic goal of increasing your liability business with most of your focus on securitized lending and mortgage business.

Be aware of the risk of using margins. It should be only a short-term fix due to its higher cost. Your clients will likely agree with Will Rogers when he said, "I'm not as interested in the return on my money as the return of my money." This is not a "dive and then check how deep the pool is." Teaching your clients and offering OWE debt strategies is a value-add to your practice that should be considered a tool in your financial belt that requires the same research, education, planning, and careful consideration as any other financial services you offer your clients.

NOTE

1. Tom Anderson. 2013. *The Value of Debt.* New York: John Wiley & Sons, Inc.

12

The Art of Asking for and Getting Introductions

You may feel awkward asking for introductions from your clients until you understand how your value helps not only your clients, but can potentially help their friends. Adopt the attitude that your clients want to help their friends be successful and feel secure about their savings and their retirement assets—and that you are the instrument for making that happen. We have an expression we teach during coaching: "Value given, value recognized." My experience has been that clients are very open to giving referrals once they see the value you have created for them. You will find that you are more comfortable and that it becomes routine after you have successfully asked a couple of clients for an introduction. Consider these five important questions when preparing to ask for an introduction:

1. Are you ready to make the ask? Do your clients and your connections know that you are open for new business? Your best referral sources may be unaware that you want to add new clients like themselves unless you let them know your practice has the capacity to grow and you do that by regularly promoting introductions at your in-person meetings. You want to ensure they are on the lookout for opportunities to proactively make introductions and regularly offer your name to a friend looking for a financial advisor. Do they see the "Open for Business" sign hanging on your door?

2. Do your sources of potential referral introductions have a working knowledge of your practice and what you offer? Most of the folks you know have a clear but narrow view of what you do for clients. The understanding is probably that you can help them grow their assets and help them save for retirement. They don't see the wide range of services you offer them. Even your best clients can have tunnel vision, focused by a single element of the most recent work you've done on their behalf. You'll receive the highest quality introductions when your sources understand what you do and how you do it. This understanding will allow the pool of potential introductions to increase. Armed with the knowledge of the impressive expanse of financial planning tools in your belt these sources of introductions will be quick to offer, "I have the perfect financial advisor for you!" when hearing that a friend is in need of financial advice.

3. Do you take time to research potential introductions? A great way to eliminate blank stares when you're seeking introductions is to till the soil before you plant seeds in your client's or COI's mind. You want your "ask" to land on fertile ground to have the best chance of producing a good crop of introductions. Before you meet with your clients and connections, identify a few folks they may know that you could suggest as possible introductions. This way you're giving them a frame of reference for offering you their best advice. This takes a little advance homework, but it is well worth the time.

4. Do you build introduction-gathering opportunities into your daily routines? Any meaningful business growth activity that is not practiced consistently can go stale. This is particularly true of introductions. When you build it into your daily routines, your chance of success grows immeasurably.

5. Do you have a script for calls that produces meaningful results? If not, create one or at least write down the highlights of your practice so you can be focused and well versed, including having your list of services ready

for the call. Work with a printed or electronic copy and make individualized notes about the call, writing down the comments the prospect makes and the questions they ask. When your call goes well and they want to move forward with their 90-Day Free Look, this documentation can be put right into their folder. If the call went well but they are still on the fence this is a record of the first call you had with them. Through trial and error your talking points will be honed and perfected producing greater results.

The premier service you provide is what created this introduction from your happy client. The importance of introductions to the growth of your practice can't be underestimated and you will discover your clients are more than willing to help. Write down what you want to say and practice it until you have it perfect.

Why Do FAs Have a Hard Time Asking for Introductions?

Cromwell Baun and Hugh Stephenson have a very successful team practice operating out of two cities, Atlanta and Dallas.
Hugh told us:

> I started in the business in '83. It was a stock by stock business. I'd make a call and try to get them to buy a stock. Then I moved to more managed money and asset allocation in the '90s. When we got to the mid to late '90s, it was clear the clients wanted "wealth management." I took several horrifically failed crash-n-burn attempts at that. Cromwell and I got together toward the end of '03. I had a client base. Cromwell had a great background in taxes. We both were committed to trying to build the planning part of the business. We had the investment part of the business.
>
> I'm not even sure we called it wealth management at that point. We had not heard of Supernova or Rob Knapp.

Even our firm was very light in giving us the tools to do financial planning for our clients. We built our practice business model pulling stuff off the internet, articles, and everything we could find over a period of a couple of years. Some of the modules, controls, and resources that we developed got absorbed by our training guys and used in the wealth management model at our firm. I thought that it was very flattering.

In 2010 I got an e-mail that Rob was going to talk about the Supernova program in Dallas. It sounded interesting to me, so I went, heard him talk and said "this is it." Supernova is the Rosetta Stone. We were signed, sealed & delivered. We worked very hard to implement the program over the year, did Supernova One, the 2nd program and some further coaching with Rob Shaffer. We followed and integrated the core of the program in every way from a Wealth Management standpoint. It has been transformational for our business.

Cromwell added:

We've had the Supernova service-model program implemented for four years now. It's been very, very positively received by our clients. They love the contact every month. They like that we're on a schedule to talk with them particularly during volatile markets. It's cut down on the reactive calls we've had previously. Clients now know we're going to talk to them in the next 1–2 weeks. That's helped us from a practice management standpoint. Clients say it's reassuring and helpful for them knowing that we are in constant communication. We have received a lot of positive feedback on the Supernova process and the 12-4-2 service model. We get a lot of unsolicited feedback about how much they've enjoyed it. It's helped keep them accountable for the things they know are on their list of things to take care of and it helps them not think about it anymore.

When those types of conversations occur, and clients mention the value they have gotten from us, it's a golden opportunity and the perfect segue to asking if there is anyone else in their circle of friends or networks of people who are like them, who might have questions about managing their wealth, are not in touch with their advisor on a regular basis or aren't getting the service they need. We let them know that we are always happy to talk with their friends and family members. We've acquired several new folks by having the ability to articulate our holistic and comprehensive service model process to existing clients who then become pretty good advocates for us.

When we specifically ask them, "Now that you've expressed your delight with the level of service and what it means for your life, is there anyone else who might enjoy this same level of service?" In some cases, they've given us specific names.

One [of a] couple who we worked with on this process for the last four years, mentioned during one of our conversations that she had a specific name of a former co-worker for us. Immediately I wanted to provide our contact information to this person. When a client has someone at the top of their mind, that's wonderful. If they say, "This is great, I don't have anyone specifically in mind, but if someone comes to me who is looking for a 2nd opinion, I'll share your name," I at least know they are thinking about us. It all flows very naturally. I had my monthly call with a doctor client, and he was talking about his practice, how they are expanding, and how they hired a couple of new doctors.

It was an opportunity to ask him "You have acknowledged all the value we've given you, we're meeting at a regularly scheduled time, and we like to take care of folks who are within our client's circle of family, friends, and other professionals. If these are folks you think would benefit from the services that we offer from a planning standpoint, we'd be happy to talk to them." The client was happy to do it and said he hadn't thought about that before but would be happy to ask them. My experience has been that I haven't received any awkward silence.

When asked if Cromwell talks to everyone he gets introductions from:

> I think our clients have a good understanding of the types of clients we would like to work with. A lot of times they will have similar assets in their network. We always tell them we're open to talking to these folks, and we're happy to help them. At the end of the day, it's up to myself and Hugh. It comes down to the client relationship. Clients sometimes have introduced us to folks who didn't meet our minimum number of assets and didn't make sense for us to work with because it didn't fit what we do for our clients. I've had some of those conversations where someone says this guy has $100K (which is well under what we would work with). I tell them I'll be glad to meet them and have a conversation with them, but it's probably not going to be a good fit. I give them my contact info, and if they feel it's not workable, I don't hear back from them.

Hugh:

> My approach is very similar. I have a set agenda. When I ask for a referral, it's at the end. The top item on the agenda is what is on their mind, questions, concerns, problems, changes in their life? I keep it very open-ended and let them talk. Overall, the experience we're trying to convey to the client is that we're 110% focused on them. Over the years, most of the time they feel like an advisor calls them when they want them to buy something. We would prefer that they have an experience with us so that when we do a regularly scheduled meeting, it's about hearing updates from them, things that are important that we think they need to know about—changes in IRA beneficiary laws, an investment move we need to make, etc. It's not a sales call.

That's the whole first part of the meeting. We then go through some fact-finding. We discuss life events, health issues, and planning for the future. For example, we might emphasize that these accounts are focused on growth, this account is from your Great Aunt Minnie, this is income only, and then we confirm investment objectives, talk about cash liquidity needs, go through any concentrated positions and real estate issues. These are checkpoints. If we come across any estate planning issues, we'll talk to an attorney. We want to develop a sense of what the relationship between their attorney and the accountant is. Is it strong or weak? Would that attorney or accountant be in the "enthusiastically endorsed" column? We want to have a sense of their hobbies and interests. We have one client who likes fishing, and he grows his worms. I usually ask in the conversation, "how are the worms?"

Usually the last thing we talk about is portfolio moves. In the whole one-hour conversation, the first 30–40 min are focused on them, their concerns, needs, questions. Then we get down to portfolio moves. Appropriately, it's a third-level concern. If we're doing the investment plan we don't want them hyper-focused on should the emerging market exposure be 8% or 10%. Then we go into the last level of questions where the referral comes. We ask them in various forms: How can we be better? What are we doing that is the most valuable thing to you? Of all the things we do, what helps you the most? We remind them we're trying to give them peace of mind.

In the first part of the conversation we try to create a personalized financial strategy that helps you have peace of mind. Unconsciously that is what people want when he or she says he or she wants an 8% rate of return. Why do you want it? Get you to your goals? If you get to your goals what does that mean to you? Then, I don't worry about it. Ultimately, that is what everybody wants.

When we talk to our client we ask them how we can be better—please tell me one thing we should keep doing, one thing we should stop doing, and one thing we should start doing. We're trying to drive this around the client experience. Close to the end, I might say, "surveys show two-thirds or three-quarters of wealthy individuals are unhappy with their financial advisor and are interested in potentially talking to another one. If you're sitting around with a group of your friends, the chances are almost certain that at least one of them is unhappy. I'm not asking you to make phone calls or go through your address book, but if the conversation comes up, please consider mentioning us if you're happy with us. We'd love to talk with them."

Ways to Create Value for Clients

When someone asks their colleagues or friends about their financial advisor what do you think is the root of the question? It is likely, "Do they make you any money? Are they easy to work with?" and probably not "What's the advantage?" How do you change that conversation from performance that you can't control to service that you can control? Your efforts save them time. They place their money with you because they trust you will handle their financial needs professionally and that you will value their time. Supernova provides the platform for this level of service through monthly contact, one-hour response, 24-hour resolution, and multi-generational planning. You also can do little things that will make a big impact on them like participating in their favorite charity's fundraisers, getting them tickets to hard-to-get events, keeping track of their travel arrangements and making sure their credit cards are working for them when it comes to benefits and privileges. As we talked about in the last chapter, an important add for them may be teaching them how to leverage debt and create opportunities to build their wealth using a cash-flow analysis.

When you are in a review meeting, this is the time to make sure what you are doing is appreciated and valued. We have talked a great deal about giving to give and not asking for anything we haven't earned.

FA Ken Shapiro uses LinkedIn to identify friends who might introduce him to someone who has recently sold their business.

He is confident that his clients and business associates know he is the right guy to help an entrepreneur who is selling his company in NYC.

FA Rod (you met him in Chapter 8) is confident that he is the right guy to help business owners and qualified prospects in my area. Confidence comes from knowing you are doing the right thing for all your clients day in and day out and knowing how to help them through life's more challenging transitions. Supernova gives you that confidence.

Here is Rod explaining it in his own words:

> We grew our practice from introductions from happy clients and introductions from their other advisors such as accountants and attorneys. I believe that if you have been in the business for five or more years and aren't doing this, you can only blame yourself. I have had a client for many years named Jeff. He introduced me to a friend with an impending liquidity event (selling their business) in the $9MM [million] range. I service approximately 100 clients with an average of $375MM in assets. This couple already had two different brokers, but they chose to bring everything to us. I worked through this with Rob in one of our sessions. The premise is, if you've been following the Supernova Process for a while, you have the right to ask your clients for introductions. Don't use the word referral, all I want is an introduction. Referral has a potentially negative connotation.

Rod continues:

> I'll role play with you. You've been a Supernova client for two or more years, and you are meeting me face to face during a review.
>
> Rod: Mr. Client, we've worked together the last five years, and I'm very grateful for you and Debbie being clients with us. I'm curious. Over the years,

what two or three things have you valued the most about what we've done for you?

Client: I like how you keep in touch with me and keep me accountable.

Rod: Anything else?

Client: You're not trying to sell me something each time we talk, and we sleep better at night knowing your team and you are helping us manage our financial life.

Rod: (I'm writing this down as they are talking.) Anything else that comes to mind?

Client: That's all I can think of right now.

Rod:

I've had people tell me they value our service. Often my older clients tell me, "If something happens to me, I know you'll take care of my spouse. I appreciate the fact that every time you call, you're not trying to sell me something. I value the performance. I value that when we have a question, you get back quickly." Depending on the moment, I will write down the information and save it. I then will say "You said I value this, this and this. I'm grateful for that. I'm curious, do you know anyone else who appreciates the same things?" They'll say things like, "Are you looking for new clients?" I'd say: "I'm looking for new clients that are just like you. And finally, is there anything that we can do better?"

Rod explains:

It's important to ask your clients what they value most. It gives you feedback on what you are doing right (and wrong) and what clients think is most important. It works. I started doing the value question within the last two years. I mark on the client's page in my CRM when I discussed this with them. I'll ask again every year or two. I also do this with prospects.

With prospects, I go right into the introduction questions while we are talking. They might ask, "How do you get paid?" I'll say, "Good question; there are five ways my firm compensates us for the services we do:

1. Commission on every transaction we make.
2. Percentage of assets. (If we actively manage assets for your family, we will charge you zero to $1\frac{1}{2}$%.) That way our interests are more aligned with yours because the only way that my compensation grows is if you add more assets or the value of your assets increase vs. a transactional relationship where whether or not you make money, I get paid. Most of my clients like the incentive. If we're holding securities and not actively managing them, we charge zero. On cash balances, we charge.0001%.
3. Our firm is the biggest marketer/seller of insured certificates of deposits of any financial institution in the country. We sell more federally issued CDs to our clients than anyone else. When you buy a $1K CD, $995 goes to the bank, and $5 goes to the firm and me. There is no cost to the client.
4. There are other services I may be able to offer you. Certain things you might do with us, like a mortgage, then I get paid. On a mortgage, for example, I assure you that you'll not only get excellent service, but you'll be able to compare whatever rate we offer to the other rates you may find for both mortgages and refinancing. We'll make sure you have a sharp pencil.
5. Finally, over time, if you're happy with us and what we do for you, I would hope and expect you would introduce us to other people just like you. That is the best way you can pay me because that means you're satisfied with what we have done for you."

It's important to keep track of the introductions you get from each client. In Rob's folder system, there is a form included you can use to write that down. After I get the names, I ask them how it would be best for me to get introduced to them. They will set up the meeting or have that person call me. If they don't do it within a week or two, I will call and remind them I would like to meet their friend.

It's important to also look at introductions from the client's perspective. Of course, once you have established a relationship with the client, they will want to show you their loyalty by introducing you to their friends. However, the client's primary reason for giving you an introduction is because they know someone who could genuinely use your help. That is why asking what they value and who do they know who would benefit from your level of service it is so important.

Let's take a moment and review the model for helping clients introduce you to potential new clients who would value you as much as they do.

In an interview recently with Bill Cates, I explained how we modified his VIPS model by adding Larry Biederman's Smart Marketing Advice Model. This addition became the "A" in VIPSA. Larry explains that the most powerful compliment you can give another human being is to ask for their advice. How many times have you received a positive result from asking for an introduction only to have the process crash on the rocks of inaction, silence, or inability to follow up? Let's see how the Advice Model solves this dilemma.

Bill Cates:

> V—Value. Question to ask the client: "What have you valued most from your experience with us in the last year?" Asking questions in threes seems to get an even better response: "What are the three most important things that you valued from our relationship this year?"

Rod uses the "What else?" question, which keeps the conversation going. Since discussing this, Rod has adapted the three-question model (Richard Wyleman) with great success. He said recently, "When I ask what the three things [clients] value from [their] experience with our team over the last year or two are, I always get three answers. I used to get one and would have to dig for more."

Bill:

> I—Important. What I would like to do now is important.
> P—Permission. With your permission, I would like to do some brainstorming. I would like to brainstorm about who else would benefit from the kind of client experience that you have had with us.

S—Suggestion. Let's start by reviewing your circles. There is your inner circle of family and closest friends. We will then progress out to your next circle of neighbors, coworkers, golfing buddies and those with whom you socialize. Finally, we move to those people that might be very qualified, but you may not know as well. They might be game-changers if they became clients. Does that sound reasonable? OK, let's start with your inner circle. (Note: if it comes to open-ended it doesn't go anywhere. The bullseye is to have a specific person in mind to discuss. At this point, you review each person quickly. We will come back to profile and prioritize them when we are finished brainstorming.)

A—Advice. Once we have circled back, prioritized our list, profiled our first prospect, we then arrange to meet them. You say, "You know your brother best, how would you suggest we meet?" This is the point in the conversation where more introductory opportunities can be lost or wasted than at any other place. We get a name and never get a meeting. In person is by far the best way to meet. The client responds that his brother lives in another state. You suggest a three-way conference call by saying to the client, "Today is Wednesday, why don't I set up a conference call for next Wednesday at this same time? Let's give you till next Monday to contact your brother. If I haven't heard from you by Monday night, I will send an email reminder. Is that OK?" Once the introductions are made, you can either arrange for a second meeting with the prospect or your client can leave you two to discuss possibilities.

This process is an important component of the Supernova Acquisition Model and can be utilized in a conversation with anyone. We know FAs who have prospects introduce them to their friends even before they become clients! To use this dialogue with your clients you first have to determine if they are comfortable with giving you an introduction. You might even provide them with a way out before prodding them for names.

You could say something like this, "Mr. Client, I know you well enough to know you enjoy helping others. And you said earlier you valued XYZ that I was doing for you. We are always looking for others to help so we can continue to grow our practice. We run a specialized practice focused on [this is where you can mention your niche] and make it our goal to help people like yourself. Would you be willing to have lunch next week to explore the relationships you have and see if any of them would be a good fit for us?" At this point, if they have someone in mind, they might jump right in with their name. Or they can agree to meet you for lunch, or they can choose to keep your relationship with them a private matter.

Just as this book was going to the publisher I had another important breakthrough. Why not add a "thank you" as the last step. That would turn VIPSA into VIPSAT. I have always had a page in the FA and client folders for introductions given and received. This page was used to write down the names of clients given and received that could potentially encourage someone to give more. Kind of a reminder. As we expanded the concept of giving to give, connecting people for the sake of really helping them, I thought more about the tracking of those introductions. We (hopefully) get so many introductions over the years we can lose track of them. Did they open an account? Who actually referred me to some clients and when was that? So I experimented with including their name and the date they were introduced and the date the account was opened. It was so well received I added it to the program. I now tell FAs to call the client on the anniversary of the opening of their account and thank them for doing business with them. More importantly, call the client or COI who **introduced** you and thank them for the introduction and let them know the new client is happy with you.

Centers of Influence and advocate clients will like you, trust you, and want to help you. They want to make both you and the friend they introduced you to happy. By calling and thanking them a year later you are reassuring them the introduction was a good idea and it worked out well for both friends. There is no better way to encourage them to repeat this behavior than to make this thank you call. A very common response to this thank you call is, "I got another friend I would like to introduce to you." Even better when you don't have to ask for anything.

Luke Wiley has been using Supernova for over ten years. He is a master of the Introduction Model and has been using it religiously for years. He even has separate appointments for brainstorming with clients over possible introductory opportunities. Today the clients are so well trained he uses an abbreviated model. In 2012, he was ranked seventh out of 7,000 advisors at his firm on Net New Clients. He has continued to receive rankings in the top 50 since then. As of the publishing of this book he was number one in his office on Net New Assets. His brother and he manage $300M. His trailing 12 months is $2,240,000, and his brother's is $710,000. Luke has four kids, works a maximum of 50 hours a week, and takes regular vacations. He says, "Time with my family is very important to me. Money can't buy you meaning." Luke has balance in his life thanks in no small part to Supernova.

Let's hear from Luke how he uses the model in conjunction with Supernova:

> My process is in Bill Cates' book *Don't Keep Me a Secret*. Bill first wrote a book called *Get More Referrals Now!* We've done some brainstorming together. He talks about my process in that book. I haven't done an orchestrated one in quite a while. Now it's just become, "Make sure you don't keep me a secret. Do you appreciate the value that we're providing?" I was in a meeting last night with a new client. I was fortunate that they were referred to me. I continue to talk about people being referred. I ask: "What is it that you value that we have done over the last year? What are some things that we can be doing better?" Then they tell you.
>
> I have one client that has been a client of mine for eight years now. I still ask her the value question: "When you think about the value we provide, what do you think is most valuable to you in working with us?" Then I let them

talk. Then you say, "Not today, but would you be open to maybe you and I setting up a conference call in a couple of weeks and maybe brainstorming to identify some other people who could benefit from the value you see in your relationship with me?" Then you reiterate the value they just said. It's interesting. Clients normally have 4-6 individuals that might need you. They don't want to keep me a secret. They want me to learn more about some of these key people in their lives. Again, "Not today, but what are your thoughts? Could we brainstorm in a couple of weeks and think of those people who could benefit from the value we provide? How does Friday at 11 am work?" Then I send them a thank you card in advance saying, "I want you to know how much I appreciate what you shared in our meeting. It means so much that you see the value we've been providing to you for years. I look forward to our call scheduled for Friday at 11 am to identify other people that you believe could benefit from the value we provide. Thanks for not keeping me a secret." They know for two weeks I am going to call.

I am very clear on my expectations. We have been in situations where we like the product the person is selling us, but we're not in the mindset to think of friends to get to them. It's essential that they know we are interested: "It's been a great meeting today. I don't want to take up any more of your time, but would you be open to brainstorming in a couple of weeks to identify other people you believe would benefit from the work we provide?" It gets them off the hook for having to change gears and start thinking about their friends. I want to be efficient. I don't want to set up lunch in 2 weeks, get into my car and meet them. I want the subject of the call to be about identifying people who would value the work we do.

I asked Luke how he talks to his current clients about the kind of clients he is looking to work with.

I'll tell you something that's helpful. Three years ago I decided, with the high level of service we provide, I will charge families under $1M 1.5% and families over $1M 1%. The minute you go over $1M you don't have to remind us, we will lower it for you. If your account later goes down under $1M, we're not going to raise the fee. What we deliver is quite unusual, and it's not fair for me to provide proactive advice to you if your account is too small to take advantage of it. We explain that to clients, so they know what we are looking for in assets. We work on investing the portfolio together, so everyone gets the advantage of our entire team focused on them. We review their plans at least once a year.

People will think about giving you $700K but then keep the rest of their account at Fidelity. We tell them to manage their account most efficiently and effectively we need everything. When they come in as a client, they see we are doing what we promised. They get a folder with your name on it. They have a dossier in the front where they can put things that are important to them. They have the whole year planned out with the date/time of when we're going to talk. It's my opinion that our retention rate is so high because of our integration and use of the Supernova process. Supernova is awesome. We owe a lot of our success to Supernova.

CHALLENGE

1. Read this chapter once a day for five days.
2. Write out your script. This will help lock it into your long-term memory.
3. Practice the VIPSAT model with a friend or your CA/CSA.
4. Use the process (VIPSAT) on five clients for two weeks. Once you have presented it ten times, it will become a part of you.

13

The Branch Manager's Role as a Supernova Multiplier

Since *The Supernova Advisor* was written, the leadership component of the Five Star Model has evolved into the single most important role. The leader is the most critical part of every team. Without their vision, drive, discipline, and ambition the team will not achieve at the level it should. What I have discovered is that leadership, on several different levels, is the key to teams successfully implementing the Supernova Process. In order to be a successful Supernova team every team member needs to be onboard and critically linked in their purpose of helping the leader succeed. If you are in a large firm you also need the support and full engagement of firm management. We have found that where upper management is fully engaged in the coaching of the Supernova Process both the leaders and the team as a whole is upwards of 30% to 50% more successful. This is another Supernova Multiplier.

In coaching thousands of teams, my team and I have noted that the difference has been remarkable when some of the cost of coaching is covered by local management or by corporate allocation. When a major firm required a local manager to be on every call the team and the manager were more engaged and had a sense of what was needed from the firm to support them. In fact, the results were dramatically better. How do you measure that?

The team adopted Supernova segmentation faster, organized the folder system and scheduling quicker, and utilized the acquisition strategies more effectively. What are the stumbling blocks these leaders navigate for the teams that we are coaching?

- Segmentation—Financial advisors presented with the idea of raising the minimum number of assets per client they manage and thus segmenting some of their smaller accounts to another advisor, don't always know where to start. They aren't sure what accounts the call center can take or how the process works. They aren't sure which FAs in the office are willing and able to handle the reassigned accounts. These issues can take weeks to resolve, which delays the process of segmentation. They can be addressed and resolved very quickly when a manager is involved, as they should know who has the capacity in their books and who would appreciate the new accounts. This shortens the cycle and frees up the FAs to move forward.
- Organization—The manager and their office assistant help the advisors and their administrative staff order the right folders in the right quantity, and are a good sounding board when the team is trying to work out the best way to have monthly contact with their clients. They also may be able to supply the team with an intern or temp to help build the folders. All this eliminates roadblocks that can disrupt them.

What can the FAs manager do to keep the team on track and have successful expectations?

- Meet with the team to follow up on the coaching call.
- Reinforce the Supernova Process.
- Facilitate the segmentation process through the firm's call center and other teams.
- Facilitate the organizational process with the use of the folders, Supernova Scheduling Tool, Five Star Model, Gameboard, and Scoreboard.
- Encourage acquisition by helping the team leader to hold the Director of Marketing accountable for the Monday Gameboard meeting.

- Support the team leader to communicate the weekly Supernova progress to the team and to coach through email or text messaging. Sending a weekly email with the homework to the coach dramatically improves the success of any business coaching practice.
- Organize a weekly meeting of all teams going through Supernova in the office. With FAs and teams at different stages of the program, they can be resources for each other as they learn and evolve, offering those further back in the process glimpses into their future.

The FA's Role as the Leader of the Team

Now that we have established the value of upper management's involvement in the Supernova transformation, what is the value of the team leader or Director of Leadership?

The Leader:
- Sets the Purpose (why), Mission (how) and Vision (what, where, when). Communicates the PMV (purpose, mission, vision) to the team at daily, weekly, monthly, quarterly, and annual meetings ensuring that all activities are aligned with the team's PMV.
- Holds teammates accountable to each other in their roles and responsibilities.
- Inspires compliance with the changes by example, encouragement, and recognition.
- Coaches all teammates individually through 12-4-2.

How do you measure team activities? We first started using a Gameboard to measure activity. The use of the Gameboard has evolved into a Giving Board. With the restrictions on cold calling, the world of acquisition has changed into relationship marketing. This new approach is a better world where the hesitant and skeptical no longer walk into any Financial Services office and ask for an advisor. Instead the new norm is to ask their closest friend; another trusted advisor, CPA or attorney; and/or their peers who they recommend as the best advisor for them and why.

Supernova fits perfectly into this world because it gives you, the FA, the confidence you are delivering a valued experience. With that confidence, you can build valued relationships with other professional advisors (CPAs, attorneys, etc.). You can also form Mastermind Groups that make sense because you have a lot to offer and can really help. All these activities are measured through the Giving Board. You no longer measure how many cold calls you make. You now measure how many introductions you give, how you helped your COIs, Mastermind Group, Niches, and clients. The Giving Board will keep track of all of that for you.

Over a 30-year period, author Shalom H. Schwartz studied Universal Values, the values and principles that matter to people in different cultures around the world. He studied thousands of adults in 12 countries. In his Theory of Basic Values, Swartz's research showed that most people rate the values of giving (benevolence), seeking to help others (preserving and enhancing the welfare of others), and providing for the general welfare in their close relationships in their top 10 of important values. In fact, this was true in more than 70 different countries around the world including the USA.

If giving is the number one universal value, and givers advance the world, then working in a team to help your clients, COIs, Niches, Mastermind Groups, and other networks is going to be good not only for you, but also for all society. It will:

- Make you feel good
- Give you energy
- Genuinely help others
- Build deeper, longer-lasting relationships and friendships
- Reinforce your credibility
- Build a barrier to entry into your practice
- Help you service your clients and grow.

Adam Rifkin, venture capitalist and serial giver, has the most extensive network on LinkedIn. Adam Grant writes:

> When Adam Rifkin helped people in his social network, the "matchers" felt it was only fair to plot his wellbeing. Adam would introduce friends to friends, help people get

jobs, help struggling entrepreneurs bring their ideas to fruition, etc. His purpose was to help. The outcome is that he is the most sought-after billionaire venture capitalists in the country.

The Giving Board takes on new energy for the entire team (see Table 13.1). Giving isn't the exclusive purview of the FA. All members of the team including the CSAs, analysts, and interns should be on the Giving Board and be given the opportunity to participate in the giving process. Who did you help this week? Can you become a serial giver? How much fun is the team having helping everyone?

Effective Leadership is Coaching

If coaching is the most effective form of leading a team, then why do so few do it? Perhaps because it takes hard work, it's tedious and time-consuming.

Let's explore that a little. Because of the incredible amount of pressure on FAs and teams to effectively manage the daily workload, it seems so much more comfortable just to tell people what to do and hope they get it done. For most team leaders it's hard enough keeping up with their work without helping others with the development of a team member. Most hope nothing goes wrong.

When you are coaching individuals on an individualized monthly basis, it creates the same environment with team members as 12-4-2 does with clients. Team members, just like your clients, save their problems and issues that aren't urgent for those 12-4-2 coaching sessions knowing they will have the opportunity to be heard at that time. The negative fallout of not doing regular check-ins with team members can be similar to that which can occur with clients. If you have a client you don't

Table 13.1   Diagram of Giving Board

Name	Client Contact	COI Contact	Niche Meetings	Community Involvement	Social Media	Master-mind Meeting	90-Day Free Look

talk to on a regular basis, there will be negative consequences. Problems don't go away. They will get bigger until they become disproportionate to the issues. The ultimate consequence is the client leaves, and/or the teams break up.

When everything in your day is scheduled, you fall into a more productive pattern. Active communication and leadership hold teams together. If done properly, the days of the annual review for all team members have passed. Instead, we recommend you have monthly coaching sessions and a quick ten-minute follow up that not only will help everyone know where they stand, but will be more effective and efficient, and will result in dramatically higher production. We often don't want coaching because we feel like we have to have all the answers. In reality, you have most of the answers already in your head. You can always ask the questions and when you get stuck—call your coach.

When you set yourself up for "regularly scheduled meetings", nothing will fall through the cracks. Having a daily ten-minute meeting is no different from what you do now when you catch up in the break room getting your morning coffee, except it is formalized and expected. Having two weekly meetings with each focusing on different areas of your practice will ensure everyone is working at their ultimate efficiency. Sample agenda for meetings:

Daily (@ 11 am)

>   What's on your mind?
>
>   Open agenda
>
>   Operations and Supernova agenda

Weekly Giving Board/Game Board (Mondays @ 9 am)

>   Activity and acquisition
>
>   FA report on giving and acquisition activity
>
>   Service Team report on giving activity

Weekly Scoreboard Meeting (Thursdays @ 4 pm)

>   Director of Planning report on weekly, monthly, YTD (year to date) results on goals set/challenges

Director of Implementation report on new investment model, changes, monthly focus

Director of Brand Management report on Supernova service and operational issues

Director of Marketing report on weekly, monthly, YTD results from acquisition strategies

Director of Leadership report on weekly, monthly, YTD results in production credits, net new assets, new relationships, change to strategy and tactics.

Each week focus on a particular area such as planning and discuss challenges and opportunities.

At these meetings, it is critical to ask the right questions. In Michael Bungay Stanier's book *The Coach Habit, Say, Less, Ask More and Change the Way You Lead Forever* he notes:

> An almost fail-safe way to start a chat that quickly turns into a real conversation is the question, "What's on your mind?" It's something of a Goldilocks question, walking a fine line, so it is neither too open and broad nor too narrow and confining. Because it's open, it invites people to get to the heart of the matter and share what's most important to them. You're not telling them or guiding them. You're showing them trust and granting them the autonomy to choose for themselves. It's a question that says, "Let's talk about the thing that matters most." It's a question that dissolves ossified agendas, sidesteps small talk and defeats the default diagnoses.

What is next? Listening. Coaching is not teaching—it's listening! The hardest thing for me to learn and most dramatic change in my style was to be quiet and listen to what others were saying. I always thought the goal was to transfer the knowledge I had to the person I was coaching when in reality, it is to help them understand their challenges and then to use my coaching knowledge to guide them to their best solutions. Usually, people know the answers to their problems, but for one reason or another they don't want to admit it. It sounds so simple, but it isn't obvious. I have heard talk show hosts take calls from viewers and the viewer usually says yes, I knew that, I didn't want to see it.

Asking "what's on your mind" worked for me and gave me a breakthrough in my coaching. We teach our Supernova advisors to have an agenda for client meetings, and the first item on the agenda is to ask them what they would like to talk about before we discuss our agenda. You are asking them: "What is on your mind?"

When you sit down with team members for ten minutes or 45 minutes ask them "What's on your mind?" You will find it to be more productive than any other conversation. After listening to their answer ask them the second question Stanier suggests: "What else?" These two questions should get you where you need to go, whether it is focusing on a current issue, managing productivity, or just establishing communication with another team member.

At the end of the conversation, you want to ensure the other person takes away what you intended and that it stays in their long-term memory instead of their short-term memory. You do that by having them articulate three things they found valuable in the session. How they answer will be an indicator of what they thought was important and thus will remember. If you want a client to remember something you said, ask them if they can repeat it. There is a higher probability they will remember it if they can repeat it. It doesn't matter what you teach if they don't retain it. Being armed with the following three questions will make you effective in any situation:

What's on your mind?

What else?

What are your three takeaways from this meeting?

The key to being a good leader is being a good coach. And the key to being a good coach is to have the desire to help the other person. Great coaches see more in people than they see in themselves, and have the ability to see potential even if the person themselves doesn't, and to help them reach it. Just remember, people will take your guidance if they believe you believe in them. Help them solve their own problems by bringing them to the solution. You do that by asking questions and helping them come up with their own solutions: "What are the options that come to mind?" "What has worked for you in the past?" "Who do you trust who has been through this same thing?"

Let's not forget that the basic premise of *The Supernova Advisor* was ritualizing an exceptional client experience for each and every client. The same model easily transitioned to the Supernova Leadership Model, which was built on Servant Leadership: checking our ego and putting all members of the team before ourselves in the DNA.

The benefits of Servant Leadership go hand in hand with the Leader Coach Model. You can't be a real coach if you don't take the time to put your team first. When asked how they feel about some great victory, every great coach always credits their players and staff for the success. I recently interviewed the top Blood Cancer Oncologist at Ohio State University and asked him that same question: "Why are you so well thought of in the medical profession? Why are you the number one of all the oncologists in the world?" Dr. Jon Byrd responded, "Because of my team." When I asked his staff the same question they said, "Dr. Byrd is an amazing person. He is wonderful to work with. We are so lucky to work with him." After spending the day at the center, I could see they were all right. They are a well-oiled machine that is at the top of the medical world. They are involved in most of the case studies all over the world, yet there was no chaos or confusion. Just plan, process, and rituals. Very impressive.

CHALLENGE

Your goal as leader is to be described with the same kind of adulation that characterizes Dr. Byrd. Do you credit your team for your successes? In other words, do you really have the Servant Leader Mindset? Make giving, helping, and coaching a part of your DNA and build a happier, healthier, and more productive life.

Enthusiastically Endorsed Resources

Client's Name				
Service	**Service Provider' Name**	**EE***	**E***	**NE***
Attorney				
Tax				
Real Estate				
Estate Planning				
Divorce				
General				
CPA				
Physicians				
FP/Concierge service				
Cardiologist				
Endocrinologist				
Neurologist				
Pulmonologists				
ENT				
Pediatrician				
Other				
Real Estate Agent				
Commercial				
Residential				
Car Salesman				
Personal Trainer				
Massage Therapist				
Housekeeper				

Client's Name				
Service	Service Provider' Name	EE*	E*	NE*
Nanny				
Pet Sitter				
Veterinarian				
Home Sitter				
Electrician				
Plumber				
Computer Consultant/Repair				
Home Repair				
Landscaper				
Country Club				
Personal Banker				
Wedding Planner/Party Planner				
Funeral Director				
Concierge Travel Service				
Limo Service				
*EE-enthusiastically endorsed; E-endorsed; NE-not endorsed				

Index